Bob Dylan and Philosophy

Popular Culture and Philosophy™

Popular Culture and Philosophy™

Bob Dylan and Philosophy

It's Alright, Ma
(I'm Only Thinking)

Edited by
PETER VERNEZZE
and
CARL J. PORTER

OPEN COURT
Chicago and La Salle, Illinois

Volume 17 in the series, Popular Culture and Philosophy™

Open Court gratefully acknowledges the permission of the artist, Milton Glaser, to use his famous Bob Dylan poster on the front cover of *Bob Dylan and Philosophy*.

To order books from Open Court, call toll-free 1-800-815-2280, or visit our website at www.opencourtbooks.com.

Open Court Publishing Company is a division of Carus Publishing Company.

Library of Congress Cataloging-in-Publication Data

To Bob Dylan

Contents

Side 2

Liner Notes

One standard that we judge artists by today is their success in appealing to our emotional nature—their ability to move us to tears or laughter, induce hope or alienation, evoke pity or rage. Painters, writers, actors, and musicians are rarely evaluated in terms of whether or not they challenge our minds. But clearly one aspect of the appeal of an artist like Bob Dylan is precisely this, his capacity to engage our intellectual nature, to speak to that part of ourselves Emerson (who was very well read, it's well known) dubbed "Man Thinking."

Granted, it's not an aptitude that currently holds much sway. In this age of Oprah, we accept as dogma both that it is not possible to feel too deeply and that it is dangerous to think too much. What is not, regrettably, reflected upon as frequently are the personal and national drawbacks of taking no time to think.

When you gonna wake up!?

Fortunately, attitudes are a-changin'. Perhaps it began a few years ago when an odd book crept its way up the bestseller list, *Sophie's World*, a novel about the history of philosophy (what next, you might ask, an opera about the development of pipe fitting?). Books like *Socrates Café, Plato, not Prozac* and *The Consolations of Philosophy*, aimed at the general reading public, have had great success. No small part in this movement was played by Open Court's Popular Culture and Philosophy series, examining shows like *The Simpsons* and *The Sopranos*, movies like *The Matrix* and *Lord of the Rings*, and even taking a swing at the national pastime, in order to explicate their obvious philosophical elements to a popular audience. As if to enshrine the new status of the discipline, *U.S. News and World Report* recently named "taking up philosophy" (even counterfeit philosophies?) as one of the fifty things to do to improve your life.

With the re-emergence of an interest in the life of the mind, it's time for an assessment of this aspect of Bob Dylan's work. Even a casual glance at the songs will reveal that Dylan's lyrics range over the same sorts of issues of value and meaning that are the proper purview of philosophy. To cite just a few examples: Tunes like "Who Killed Davey Moore?" and "The Lonesome Death of Hattie Carroll," in their attempt to define the terms 'good' and 'bad' (quite clearly, no doubt, somehow) bring into play ethical notions of responsibility and justice; the numerous protest songs such as "Masters of War" concern themselves, as does political philosophy, with thinking 'bout the government; many of the lyrics from the Christian period albums explicitly address issues of faith and salvation familiar to philosophers of religion, who often wonder just whose side God is on; and from "Desolation Row" to "It's Not Dark Yet" the topic of whether every moment of existence seems like some dirty trick, dealt with by existentialism, finds ample expression. Finally, let's not forget that not only the princess and the prince, but also Aristotle, Heidegger, and a few other philosophers, discuss what's real and what is not.

This does not, of course, mean that Bob Dylan is a philosopher, even if the professors do like his looks. The title, after all, is *Bob Dylan and Philosophy*. It suggests at most a relationship between the two, and not necessarily one of identity. As with the other volumes in the Popular Culture and Philosophy series, all that is asserted is that the focus of the work—be it the *Simpsons*, the *Sopranos*, or the *Matrix*—serves as a jumping off point for a discussion of philosophical issues, and that the exploration of these philosophical issues enriches our understanding of the subject. That Dylan raises topics of philosophical interest is something evident to even the most casual Dylan fan (is there such a thing?), and if you have any doubt, simply skim the table of contents.

While the essays are not without a consideration of topics other than the lyrics, the attempt to link the songs to a twenty-five hundred year old history of rational argumentation has compelled us to focus this book on an analysis of Dylan's words. For those interested, there are several excellent treatments of the musical component of Dylan's work, for example, Paul Williams's masterful three-volume *Bob Dylan: Performing Artist*. By contrast, this is the first book to treat Dylan's work solely from a philosophical standpoint; it is the *logos*, or the element of Dylan's art that appeals above all to our rational capacity, as opposed to the *muthos*, or the aspects that primarily address other parts of our nature, that dominates here, and we make no apologies (though, in case you feel like it, now is the time for your tears).

After reading these essays, we hope you'll concur with us that something is happening here—and we think we know what it is. Universities have taught courses on Dylan for quite some time. Yet with the publication of Christopher Ricks's magisterial study of Dylan's literary prowess, *Dylan's Vision of Sin*, a case is beginning to be made for a reassessment of Dylan's role in relation to the intellectual community some thirty-five years after he received an honorary doctorate from Princeton. We offer this book as another exhibit for the prosecution (or is it the defense?) of this case. Ricks has put to rest any debate over Dylan's status as poet. The only question left to consider is whether he is a poet of sufficient merit and intellectual heft to deserve a place, not merely on the list of great American performers, but among the pantheon of uniquely American minds alongside such notables as Emerson, Thoreau, Whitman, Melville, Twain, Dickinson, Dubois, O'Neill, Kerouac, and Ginsberg. Like these icons, Dylan has explored the nature of reality—metaphysical, ethical, political, and religious reality—in a substantial body of work, he has communicated his vision of the world through a recognized artistic medium, and he has provoked his audience to thoughtful reflection about their lives and their connection to the universe—and has accomplished all of this in a distinctly American voice.

Can this really be the end? No, actually, it's just the beginning. So kick back, put on your favorite Dylan album, and get ready to learn a little about philosophy, and perhaps even a bit about Dylan.

Acknowledgments

We love Bob Dylan's work and we love philosophy. When we first conceived the project for this book, we were concerned that we might not be able to do justice to Dylan and at the same time do justice to philosophy, but as the volume took shape, we were first relieved, and then exultant. We are above all grateful to the authors of these chapters. For combining their passion for Dylan with their knowledge of philosophy, they deserve a standing ovation. The term "labor of love" is doubtless overused, but we can think of no better phrase to describe their efforts.

But the book would never have seen the light of day without the support of the immaculately frightful David Ramsay Steele at Open Court. It has also greatly benefited from the numerous suggestions and careful nurturing of Bill Irwin.

Jeff Rosen's office, in particular his assistant Lynne Okin Sheridan, could not possibly have been more helpful in facilitating our securing permission to quote Dylan's lyrics. May they stay forever young. (Jeff and Lynne, we mean, not the lyrics, which we all know are much younger now than ever.) We'd like to thank Carol Olson, James Stewart, and Dave Truncillito for helping to get the volume off the ground. Our colleagues at Weber State University were indispensable in the process. A special thanks to Richard Greene and Mikel Vause. Claire Hughes and Ashley Remkes provided editorial and secretarial assistance. Others who deserve special mention include: Pamela Hall, Robert and Ann Jensen, Jim and Norma Porter, Tricia Porter, Michael Schumacher, Craig Smith, Chris Swartz, and Mary Vernezze.

Material from the following has been reproduced by gracious courtesy of Special Rider Music. All rights reserved. International copyright preserved. Reprinted by permission.

Absolutely Sweet Marie. Copyright © 1966 by Dwarf Music; renewed 1994 by Dwarf Music.

Side 1

1
Planet Waves: Dylan's Symposium

DOUG ANDERSON

> Love always sleeps rough, on the ground, with no bed, lying in doorways and by roads in the open air; sharing his mother's nature, he always lives in a state of need. On the other hand, taking after his father, he schemes to get hold of beautiful and good things. He's brave, impetuous, and intense; a formidable hunter, always weaving tricks; he desires knowledge and is resourceful in getting it; a lifelong lover of wisdom; clever at using magic, drugs and sophistry.[1]

What happens when you put six men in a room and ask them what love means? No doubt a number of good punch lines might follow, but this was a question asked by Plato some twenty-five hundred years ago in his dialogue *The Symposium*. A symposium was a Greek drinking party in which the men lay on couches and, following a specific hierarchical order, took turns in singing contests or in discoursing on a subject chosen by the group. The talk was interspersed with music and drinking rituals. One can imagine this discussion with the gang from *Cheers* or any selection of off-beat intellectuals, say, Norman Mailer, Jack Kerouac, and Bertrand Russell.

Bob Dylan's *Planet Waves*, like *The Symposium*, constitutes a set of "discourses" on what love means, each song manifesting a different possibility. Not surprisingly, Plato's tales of the mean-

---

[1] Plato, *The Symposium* (New York: Penguin, 1999), 203d. Hereafter cited parenthetically in text.

ing of love focus initially on the local Greek practices in the late
fifth century B.C.E., and Dylan's songs provide an American take
on the experiences of love of late twentieth century American
males. In both cases, the basic versions of love are obvious to
those already involved with these respective cultures. But the
final judgment on genuine love is, at least for the general public, initially surprising in both cases. Love in its highest form is,
in the end, a desire or passion for truth and beauty that transcends our immediate life experiences. It is an erotic desire for
the unattainable.

Plato's *Symposium* takes place in 416 B.C.E. at the home of
Agathon, a successful Athenian playwright. As in most of Plato's
dialogues, the central figure is his mentor Socrates, who wrote
no works of his own. Among those in attendance are Phaedrus,
an aspiring poet who sees the party as an opportunity to
enhance his social standing; Erixymachus, an intellectually-
minded physician; Aristophanes, the comic dramatist who sati-
rized Socrates in his play *The Clouds*; and Alcibiades, a young
and impetuous Greek general whose life Socrates had once
saved in battle. As a group they are well experienced in the
ways of Athenian love.

The *Symposium's* story of love develops from basic descriptions of human physical attraction to accounts of more spiritual
and intellectual attractions. As the party develops each speaker
tells a story of love that is then trumped by the next speaker.

Phaedrus begins by acknowledging that love is the origi-
nating god who inspires courage and commitment. Pausanias,
accepting the basic tale of inspiration, proceeds to draw a distinction between common and heavenly love. The former is for
inferior men who are attracted to woman, especially by the
lure of their bodies. Heavenly love is instead directed toward
boys and involves an attraction for the mind or soul. The doc-
tor Erixymachus, agreeing that love is better when directed
toward the mind or soul, shifts the discussion to focus on
love's ability to create a balance in life and to, for example,
enable friendship. He rejects the notion that love is a one-way
street.

Pursuing this sense of balance, Aristophanes the playwright
tells an elegant myth in which humans are whole at birth but are
then split into two. Love is the resulting desire for wholeness
that leads us to seek our other half: "It draws the two halves of

our original nature back together and tries to make one out of two and heal the wound in human nature" (*Symposium*, 193d). The sense of consummation and the complementarity of the love relationship are key features of this myth. Agathon, the host who had two days earlier won the tragic competition at the Lenaean festival, then stirs the pot by introducing the idea that a "definition" is needed, not just myths and stories. He wants a more philosophical take, which we are to expect of Socrates whose turn is next. Surprisingly, Socrates "defines" by recalling a conversation about the nature of love he had had with a wise "woman from Mantinea" by the name of Diotima. In Socrates's tutelage by Diotima, Plato moves away from human love to a more divine conception. The object of love is no longer a particular person but the beauty and immortality of ideas; these are the ideas about which Plato is writing to us, his readers. Thus, the highest love is a sort of philosophical *eros* in which we seek the truths we can never fully have.

Dylan sings of a similar sort of ascension, and like Plato leaves us thinking about what it is he's doing in performing the songs of the album. His ultimate eros is not for the characters and events in his songs, but for the performance itself. *Planet Waves* brims with "guy" songs, all concerning love, all American in flavor.

The attendants at Dylan's symposium-like recording sessions of November 5th, 6th, and 9th, 1973, are the members of the band which is, for the most part, the Band—Robbie Robertson, Rick Danko, Levon Helm, Richard Manual, and Garth Hudson. Having undertaken to sing their own version of Americana rock on their first two albums, they are fitting contributors to the story of American love. Unlike the attendees of Plato's symposium, their interactions are more musical and poetic than intellectual, and this too is appropriate for Dylan's final suggestion about love's meaning. Though it is mere conjecture on my part, it isn't hard to suppose that spiritual lubricants may have been employed in the recording sessions just as they were at the symposium. The trajectory of ascension that Dylan offers runs from puppy love to the eros of his own creative work. His angle of vision is decidedly masculine and thus causes us to be on guard for traces of narrowness; his final view of love, like Plato's, remains open to feminist correction and revision.

Young Love and Lovin' the One You're With

American love begins with the sweetness of a teenage guy's crush on a young girl. Desire is front and center, pure and simple, though it is focused on innocence rather than sexuality. It's the springtime or summertime romance that nostalgia later looks back on with fondness. The pop sound of "You Angel You" marks this first level of love. The insight is that love involves both desire and incompleteness. The lover lacks something that is in some way fulfilled by the beloved. This puppy love is shot through with naivety and blindness; it makes the lover sing:

> You angel you
> You got me under your wing
> The way you walk and the way you talk
> I feel I could almost sing

The last line is nicely appropriate to Dylan but also captures a truth about most young lovers. They engage in a love of spontaneity that reveals little self-awareness and even less awareness of the actual nature of the beloved. The desiring youth exemplifies the cliché that "love is blind."

"You Angel You" reveals Dylan's ability to match the Bee Gees, Herman's Hermits, and Tommy James and the Shondells with a quality pop love song. The simplicity of lyric and tune nicely accompany the simplicity of the youthful crush. We listeners don't need to be told what kind of love it is—we hear it and recognize that it is *not* genuine love. It's a form we leave behind and move forward from. In the *Symposium,* Plato tells us that Love is the offspring of the gods *Poverty* and *Resource,* and it seems likely that Dylan, as folk poet, is experientially familiar with both. The second level, or what I will call adult eros, seems to draw on this experiential familiarity—the singer of "On a Night Like This," "Tough Mama," and "Hazel" seems, as Jimi Hendrix might have put it, more "experienced." We hear a shift in voice as Dylan moves closer to the emotive pitch of Jim Morrison, Janis Joplin, and Hendrix. The love that is born of resource and poverty is more aware and moves to the adult level of sexual desire. We encounter erotic love—a need to be fulfilled *by* and perhaps *with* another. On *Planet Waves,* Dylan's American eros is most explicitly heterosexual and stands in place of the hetero- and homosexual relations described in the *Symposium*. This leaves open a second avenue of possible correction and revision of Dylan's story of love.

"On a Night Like This" pictures a one night stand of pure, playful bliss:

> Let the four winds blow around this old cabin door
> If I'm not too far off
> I think we did this once before
> There's more frost on the window glass
> With each new tender kiss
> But it sure feels right
> On a night like this

"Hazel" and "Tough Mama" suggest more involved relationships, but ones still focused on sexual compatibility and straightforward physical desire. Physicality is what's at stake. As does Plato, Dylan points out that most such affairs are short-termed. Like the bodies involved, physical eros ignites and then burns out. Although they are more informed affairs and often outlive puppy love, they have no permanence and yield no possibility of immortality for the lovers. The adultness and added sophistication reveal more self-awareness, and the relationship seems more mutual or co-operative than teen love. Nevertheless, physical eros is ultimately incomplete, insufficient, and unsatisfying.

You Ain't Goin' Nowhere

Ascending further, Dylan and the Band project two higher versions of love: "true love," the eros of complementarity and *agape*, the cherishing love that made its way into American culture through a variety of Christian traditions. One of the noticeable features of the two previous types of love—puppy love and adult eros—is their self-directedness and, perhaps, selfishness. The innocent, youthful lover is amazed by his own feelings and focuses on them. The beloved is looked on as an object that serves as the cause of these unusual new feelings, a phenomenon advertisers have long since learned to take advantage of. Adult eros, on the other hand, focuses on self-satisfaction—on achieving some basic physical pleasure. Whatever "sweet nothings" are offered to the beloved, the cash value is the proverbial "good time." Drawing on the double entendres of the blues, Dylan opens "Tough Mama" with the singer's sexual aims:

> Tough mama
> Meat shakin' on your bones
> I'm gonna go down to the river and get some stones
> Sister's on the highway with that steel drivin' crew
> Papa's in the big house, his workin' days are through
> Tough Mama,
> Can I blow a little smoke on you?

And in "Hazel" the singer opens with an understated compliment but then comes to the point:

> Hazel, dirty blonde hair
> I wouldn't be ashamed to be seen with you anywhere
> You got something I want plenty of
> Ooh, a little touch of your love

In both songs, the singer is focused on his own pleasure, trying to coax his partner to get "in the mood."

To move beyond puppy love and physical eros, love must overcome its inner directedness, its selfishness. In higher forms of love, as Plato suggested, some attention must be devoted to the beloved. Agape is the traditional mode of love that does just this, and despite the sexual liberality of the latter half of the twentieth century, agape remained an American ideal. For the Greeks agape was a cherishing concern of a superior for an inferior and did play at least a cameo role in homosexual relations between older and younger men, as Pausanias suggests. Later, in Christian traditions agape came to define God's love for his creatures. Drawing on both of these models, agape is well exemplified in a parent's love for his or her children. Both versions of Dylan's "Forever Young"—the playful rock and roll version and the softer, lullaby version—fully capture the spirit of this cherishing love. In an American vein such agape is almost always thought of as wishing some form of success for one's offspring. And, though Dylan presents it in a charming way, the song's very theme states what most Americans seem to want— a non-Dorian Gray perpetual youth. Agape almost forgets the lover in its emphasis on the life of the beloved:

May your wishes all come true

. . .

May your heart always be joyful
May your song always be sung
May you stay forever young

In his agapastic ode to his children, Dylan actually appeals to the Greek virtues that have filtered down to American culture. He hopes for his children to be righteous, true, courageous, strong, busy, and swift.

Some believe agape, precisely because it ignores the lover's aims, is the highest form of human love. One's own desires are set aside to pursue the fulfillment of another's desires. However, while agape is the love of Dylan the father, it is not the love of Dylan the poet who both writes and performs the song. It's difficult to tell whether agape or the next form of love, "true love," stands higher in the eyes of the American populus. But on *Planet Waves* "true love" or complementarity seems a notch higher in the poet's eyes simply by virtue of the seriousness and intensity of the songs in which it appears, especially "Wedding Song." Moreover, in being aimed exclusively at the beloved's needs, agape is susceptible to a kind of martyrdom that may not be healthful for the beloved or the lover. We need only consider the doting parent or the pushy soccer mom or football dad. The developmental nature of cherishing concern leaves us with serious questions. When do, or should, children return agapic love to their parents? Is self-interest somehow continually deferred? This may seem appealing to the cultural Calvinism inherited by many Americans, but it can lead to a grimness and resentment that, at some point, is difficult to identify as "loving."

What I'm calling "true love," on the other hand, must balance eros and agape. Ideally, this is done insofar as one's own desire is met in the fulfillment of the beloved's desire. This mutuality or complementarity suggests the superiority of this mode of love to those we've examined so far. The American version of this is the true love to be found in the "marriage" of a man and a woman. Admittedly, the mutuality is distorted when "marriage" is added simply because the American wedding—certainly in 1973—includes the imbalance of obedience of wife to husband, suggesting further need for feminist revision. If we lay this concern aside for the moment, we can see some of the details of true love Dylan presents in "Wedding Song."

True love is a consummated desire, achieved in the American mythos through marriage—legal or otherwise. In its erotic blush it counts on the very litany of clichés that Dylan employs: the husband loves the wedded wife "more than time and more than love / . . . more than the stars above." The consummatory or complete nature of this love is achieved in two ways: through its espoused eternality and through the complementary nature of the couple. An eternal love, as Plato also suggested, precludes other competing loves, in this way overcoming other desires—eros remains but is now directed toward one person indefinitely. As Dylan puts it: "My thoughts of you don't ever rest, they'd kill me if I lie / I'd sacrifice the world for you and watch my senses die." And later in the song: "And if there is eternity, I'd love you there again." This aim of permanency and unconditionality bring true love to a higher level than either puppy love or physical eros. This form is at once more serious and more tender. Two disclaimers in the song, however, hint at what I think (and I believe Dylan the poet thinks) is a weakness in this mode of love: "It's never been my duty to remake the world at large / Nor is it my intention to sound a battle charge." The true lover is willing to "sacrifice the world" for his beloved. This may be true enough of those of us who live in ordinary fashion, but it hardly seems true of the poet who awakens a culture to its own existential problems. The point is that in true love the love of an individual is made to transcend a concern for the larger world. We will return to this point in a bit.

The second aspect of true love's completeness is the complementary nature of the lovers' relationship. In the *Symposium*, Aristophanes described love as the finding of one's "soul mate," one's "other half" who had been separated at the origin. In "Wedding Song" Dylan directly mimics the Greek story:

Oh can't you see that you were born to stand by my side
And I was born to be with you, you were born to be my
     bride
You're the other half of what I am, you're the missing piece
And I love you more than ever with a love that doesn't
     cease

Again, true love stands above other loves by completing a pre-destined event in nature—the complementary lovers find each other and are wedded. And since their relationship was "meant to be," their getting together enhances the life of each; they are *equally* lover and beloved. Thus, true love, if achieved, over-comes the defect of focusing one's energies exclusively on one-self or on one's beloved. Such love is a mutual transaction between lovers. In Dylan's words: his beloved made his "life a richer one to live," she "taught [him] how to give," and she taught his "eyes to see." These are precisely the clichés we all turn to in describing true love. Such a satisfying eros seems dif-ficult to improve upon; it includes caring, physical satisfactions, mutual sacrifice, *and* it aims at eternity. But as Diotima, through Socrates's memory, argues in the *Symposium*, a higher form does seem possible, but only if we move beyond persons as the objects of love. Following the tracks and the performance of *Planet Waves*, I believe we can find a similar higher form within the American mythos.

Hollywood—especially the Hollywood of the 1950s—makes it hard to move past true love as the defining pinnacle of all love. Even when the love encounters are unsuccessful, the ideal aim is always to find "true love" between a man and a woman that eventuates in a traditional marriage. Even for a room full of men like Dylan and the Band, the lure of this ideal is tremendous; how else could Dylan write "Wedding Song" without a trace of irony? Likewise, the Greek men at Plato's symposium have difficulty moving beyond the leading form of love in their own culture. Pausanias, for one, makes fun of the love practices of non-Athenians. For rhetorical effect, Plato introduces Diotima to lead Socrates toward the higher form, philosophical eros or the human desire for truth and wisdom. Diotima goes on to demonstrate the weakness of any love less than this. What "love" *is*, in its highest form, seems to lead us beyond the true love of any finite human couple. *Planet Waves* suggests a way to proceed in this direction but within the American context.

Love Minus Zero, No Limit or Going, Going Gone

The tensions that arise among Dylan's songs on *Planet Waves* show the still transient nature of true love despite its purported claim to eternality. The juxtaposition of "Wedding Song" and "Dirge" reminds us of a truism. What in one mood stands as true love can turn, in some cases almost spontaneously, in the direction of "Dirge's" bitterness: "I hate myself for lovin' you." Whatever else true love is, it is finite; the lover and the beloved die and their love, even if maintained for a lifetime, is only kept alive after that in memory, song, and story. Dylan and the Band's performance on *Planet Waves,* even as it describes the various forms of love, gives life to a mode of eros that *can* transcend a particular life, a particular generation, or a particular history.

The tension between "Never Say Goodbye" and "Going, Going Gone" takes us a step further. "Never Say Goodbye" is the classic, hopeful line of the true lover—"never" suggests the possibility of forever. But in "Going, Going Gone" we get the hard truth of the American male's worried answer. Instead of never saying goodbye, the lover says:

> I been hangin' on threads
> I been playin' it straight
> Now, I've just got to cut loose
> Before it gets late

Too late for what, we wonder? The true love that binds one to a single person prohibits development of the final mode of love. It gets in the way. One hopes to find "everything," full complementarity, in the beloved other, but this complementarity almost invariably fails. As lovers, we encounter the finitude of the other and vice versa; barriers are laid in the way of further growth. It was Socrates's awareness of this truth that so frustrated the young Alcibiades, who, on a drunken binge, crashes the party late and accuses Socrates of ignoring him when they slept together. In Greek life, the older Socrates should have been the "lover" and Alcibiades the beloved. Moreover, Socrates should have wanted physical consummation with Alcibiades. But Socrates, well aware of the limitations of any human beloved, stood fast with philosophical eros; desire for truth outweighed any short-term arrangements of the young Alcibiades. His was an eros that transcended human finitude. As Diotima taught Socrates, "the object of love must be immortality" (*Symposium,* 207a), and it must be actively pursued: "It's to achieve immortality that everything shows this enthusiasm [for its offspring, physical or intellectual], which is what love is" (208b).

In "Going, Going Gone" Dylan, like Socrates, turns to a wise woman for advice concerning love:

Grandma said, "Boy, go and follow your heart
And you'll be fine to the end of the line
All that's gold isn't meant to shine
Don't you and your true love ever part"

The irony here is that the song is about leaving a human beloved, a "true love," behind—a particular relationship is brought to an end. Yet one must not part from one's real "true love." Following one's heart suggests, then, that the true love is not a person but a way of life—a life in which one must always be going away from relationships that interfere with it, just as Socrates avoids Alcibiades. A similar note is sounded in "Something There Is About You." There the protagonist is on the way toward American true love, but stops short: "I could say I'd be faithful, I could say it in one sweet, easy breath / But to you that would be cruelty and to me it would surely be death." Dylan too sees the constraints of loving in finitude. This brings us back to a thought we deferred earlier—what is Dylan's truest love?

If we step back from the individual songs of the album and consider instead their creation and their performance, we get a quick glimpse of what Dylan loves. His love is not directed at any particular persons but at immortality through the works he creates. Like *The Symposium*, *Planet Waves* is about love; but like *The Symposium* it is also created as an act of love. Dylan, like Plato, is out to "affect the day," as Thoreau put it. He's no simple house husband or innocent young lover; he's a poet driven by eros to create beauty and truth. *Planet Waves* appeared shortly before Dylan's master-piece *Blood on the Tracks* and shortly after he had been panned for having lost his creative edge. The album is a poetic rebirth whose opening liner note proclaims: "Back to the Starting Point!" It is a symposium on love meant to display once again Dylan's own passion for poetic creation. As Diotima put it: "Love's function is giving birth in beauty both in body and mind" (206c).

In considering the passion for creation as the highest form of love or eros, we stand in danger of confusing fame-seeking with poetic creativity. The passionate poet—Shakespeare, Blake, Byron, Williams, Dickinson—does acquire fame, but only as a result of giving birth to immortal works. Dylan never stuck to a formula for making money or achieving fame. His career is marked by change, a gambling nature, failure, and rebirth—his performance on *Planet Waves* and elsewhere exemplifies the passion for truth and beauty, not the insecurity of a fame seeker or money chaser. Fame and money are not the ultimate objects of Dylan's love. Parents seek to live on in their children; poets live on in their work. The streaker in Yankee Stadium and the blue tu-tu guy at an Olympic event are seekers of fame. They achieve nothing that lasts. Artists seek immortality through their artistic offspring, and this was Dylan's game from the moment he left the cold of Minnesota for the possibilities of New York. "People look enviously at Homer and Hesiod and other good poets," Diotima tells Socrates, "because of the kind of children they have left behind them, which provide them with immortal fame and remembrance by being immortal themselves" (209d). In our American world, we look enviously at Dylan, not for his money and fame, but because his musical offspring speak for us truths that we have been unable to articulate.

As do Plato and Socrates, Dylan must abandon other relationships when they interfere with his one true love. This sounds callous to the champions of agape and traditional marriage, who want to portray the commitment to poetic creation as selfish. That strikes me as "sour grapes" at best. Notice that we seem willing to accept the celibacy of those who "marry" God, but we want to denigrate those who are wedded to realizing beauty and truth. The passionately creative folk-poet is not merely selfish and does not abandon the rest of the world but brings to it some truth, beauty, and wisdom that we all can experience. Poets like Dylan aim their desire not at themselves but at the works they bring to life. I can easily imagine living on far less money than I have; I do not like to imagine a world without Dylan's songs. If "true love" achieves a kind of limited consummation, poetic eros aims to transform the world itself. This is what Diotima wanted Socrates to see, that the highest form of love yields treasures for the world: "Wisdom and other kinds of virtue: These are brought to birth by all the poets and by those craftsmen who are said to be innovators" (209a). Music, poetry, and philosophy are not the useless practices that guidance counselors tell us they are; they are the divine gifts of those who love in the highest way possible, and we fans—fanatics—both experience and understand the cash value of these gifts.

2

"I Used to Care, but Things Have Changed": Passion and the Absurd in Dylan's Later Work

RICK ANTHONY FURTAK

Those who admire Bob Dylan's entire career as a songwriter are used to hearing other people complain that his later albums are filled with cynical and pessimistic lyrics. And so they are—but this is no reason for anyone to disdain all of the recordings Dylan has made since the sixties. On the contrary, one of the virtues of his later work is its exploration of these gray areas—that is, bleak emotional landscapes and states of mind which are only a few shades removed from an absolutely black despair. At his darkest of moments, Dylan shows us something about the possibility of finding hope in a blighted world, and he even considers how one might continue to live without hope if necessary. In doing so, he makes a valuable contribution to the literature of the existential tradition, which is represented by such philosophers as Søren Kierkegaard (1813–1855) and Albert Camus (1913–1960).

Existential Attunement to *Blood on the Tracks*

Existential philosophy is preoccupied with questions about the meaning of life, and it takes very seriously the experience of anguish or disenchantment in which that meaning is at issue. This is not due to a perverse taste for unpleasant moods, but because such moods are viewed as revealing certain truths about the human condition. It's fully legitimate, Camus suggests, to ask whether or not life is worth living—indeed, he calls this "the fundamental question of philosophy."[1]

---

[1] Albert Camus, *The Myth of Sisyphus and Other Essays* (New York: Vintage,

Although we are often surrounded by advertisements "proclaiming from every wall that life is not tragic," this kind of insistent optimism seems to Camus "like a bad joke in today's world."[2]

Turning our eyes away from the harshest features of existence prevents us from living on authentic terms. Along similar lines, Kierkegaard suggests that "a person who himself has become unhappy" may be in a unique position "to help others who are capable of realizing happiness."[3]

In a radio interview following the release of his album *Blood on the Tracks*, Dylan remarked that he couldn't understand why so many people were enthralled with such a painful collection of songs—but he could have found in Aristotle's *Poetics* an account of why this album would have so many fans.[4]

It is not because we enjoy pain, but because we value works of art that help us understand life by "telling it like it is," portraying the sort of things that happen to people similar to ourselves. This is why, when we are in the audience at a Dylan concert, we often feel as if we are hearing the story of our own lives.

According to Camus, our sense of the absurd arises out of the encounter between the human need for meaning and "the unreasonable silence of the world": in other words, we desire that our lives make sense, that they not seem vain and insignificant.[5]

But "one day the 'why' arises and everything begins in that weariness tinged with amazement."[6]

This condition, in which the self has fallen away from its meaningful engagement with the world, is described by Camus as "essentially a divorce."[7]

1991), p. 3.
[2] Camus, *Lyrical and Critical Essays* (New York: Vintage, 1970), pp. 185, 351.
[3] *The Diary of Søren Kierkegaard* (New York: Citadel Press, 1993), p. 58. Camus agrees, affirming that one "does not discover the absurd without being tempted to write a manual of happiness." *Myth of Sisyphus*, p. 122.
[4] Interview with Mary Travers, cited by Howard Sounes in *Down the Highway: The Life of Bob Dylan* (New York: Grove Press, 2001), p. 285. See Aristotle, *Poetics*, 1449a. Kierkegaard discusses this text in *Stages on Life's Way* (Princeton: Princeton University Press, 1988), p. 460.
[5] Camus, *Myth of Sisyphus*, p. 28.
[6] Camus, *Myth of Sisyphus*, p. 13.
[7] Camus, *Myth of Sisyphus*, p. 30.

The image ought to sound curiously appropriate to those who are familiar with *Blood on the Tracks*, the first of Dylan's albums to be dominated by a feeling of absurdity:

> She was married when we first met
> Soon to be divorced
> I helped her out of a jam, I guess
> But I used a little too much force
> We drove that car as far as we could
> Abandoned it out West
> Split up on a dark sad night
> Both agreeing it was best ("Tangled Up in Blue")

What better illustration could there be of "the divorce between the mind that desires and the world that disappoints" than the narrative of a tragic love affair?[8]

After all, love is identified by one existential philosopher as the basis of a person's "many-sided interest in the things of this world," and others (such as Kierkegaard) would agree.[9]

Martin Heidegger (1889–1976) uses the word "care" to refer to this attitude, disposition, or frame of mind that grounds our emotional involvement in the world.[10]

Regardless of what language we prefer to use, we can easily tell that the voice behind these lyrics from the mid-1970s is that of someone who has loved or cared about certain things in life to such a degree that he is liable to be utterly devastated by their loss. The passionate attachments that once held the speaker's world together as a meaningful whole are now tearing him apart, and he's going out of his mind, "With a pain that stops and starts / Like a corkscrew to my heart," as he sings in "You're a Big Girl Now." The divorce that weighs upon him is not the one alluded to in the above lines from "Tangled Up in Blue," but one of more cosmic proportions.

---

[8] Camus, *Myth of Sisyphus*, p. 50.

[9] Max Scheler, *Selected Philosophical Essays* (Evanston: Northwestern University Press, 1973), p. 98. See also Kierkegaard, *Works of Love* (Princeton: Princeton University Press, 1995), p. 215.

[10] Martin Heidegger, *Being and Time* (Albany: SUNY Press, 1996), pp. 180–81. On "love" and "care" in Kierkegaard's writings, see M. Jamie Ferreira, *Love's Grateful Striving* (New York: Oxford University Press, 2001), pp. 43–44.

"If the world is a matter of indifference" to someone who feels that life is absurd, Camus argues, "it is because he has an idea of something that is not or could not be indifferent to him."[11]

For Dylan's narrator, it is because a love that once gave him sustenance has withdrawn from his life that he now finds himself drifting through the ruins of an empty world. As he reflects upon what has been lost, he feels as if "nothing really matters much" ("Shelter from the Storm"). Having suffered a disappointment of the most intimate kind, the speaker has developed what another existential philosopher calls "the tragic sense of life" more generally.[12]

He woke up, the room was bare, he didn't see her anywhere; then, after telling himself that he "didn't care" about her departure, he felt an "emptiness inside" ("Simple Twist of Fate")— which may indicate that his ability to care about anything whatsoever has been damaged. If we imagine that this woman meant more to him than anyone else in the world, and that his care for her influenced the way he lived, then it is reasonable for him to feel as if a void has opened up within and around him, as if he is no longer on solid ground. For who is he, without his care for her? And what good is a world from which she is absent?[13]

The character in this drama has experienced the negation of his own being, and has watched the world turn into a meaningless chaos.

And when finally the bottom fell out
I became withdrawn
The only thing I knew how to do
Was to keep on keepin' on ("Tangled Up in Blue")

What was predicted in an earlier song ("If Not for You") has been fulfilled: the sky has fallen and he cannot see the floor.

---

[11] Camus, *The Rebel* (New York: Vintage, 1991), p. 7.

[12] Miguel de Unamuno, *The Tragic Sense of Life* (New York: Dover, 1954).

[13] See Jean-Luc Marion, *God without Being* (Chicago: University of Chicago Press, 1991), p. 136. Christopher Ricks discusses a similar theme in connection with a different song in *Dylan's Visions of Sin* (New York: HarperCollins, 2003), pp. 125–26.

Because of this sudden change of fortune, Dylan's narrator is appalled by the disparity between his framework of expectations and the sad reality of his circumstances. Lacking any reason to go on, he resolves to keep on going anyway—although, perhaps, without the type of passion that animates a person who is wholeheartedly engaged with the world. When the meaning of life has been obscured, life itself remains, and one must either commit suicide or else figure out how to endure those times when, as Kierkegaard says, "One cannot see the meaning of things and waits in vain for connectedness."[14]

Perverse as it may sound, there is some truth in Camus's assertion that "continuity in despair can give birth to joy," even though he adds that it would be more noble "to persevere in love" if possible.[15]

"Brownsville Girl" and Infinite Resignation

Twelve years after *Blood on the Tracks*, in a song co-authored with Sam Shepard, Dylan returns to the metaphor in which a drive on the highway stands for a relationship in time. The narrator's long rambling lines, and his enjoyment in going down the road, seem to celebrate the very fact of perseverance—even as he is moved to recollect other travels with another love whose bittersweet history is still vivid in his mind:

> Well, we're drivin' this car and the sun is coming up over the
> Rockies
> Now I know she ain't you, but she's here and she's got that
> dark rhythm in her soul
> But I'm too over the edge and I ain't in the mood anymore
> to remember the times when I was your only man
> And she don't want to remind me—she knows this car would
> go out of control ("Brownsville Girl")

Between the "she" who is riding in the passenger seat and the absent "you" who is being addressed lies all the tragic ambigu-

---

[14] *Works of Love*, pp. 132–33. Camus praises the artist who "rejects the world on account of what it lacks and in the name of what it sometimes is" in *The Rebel*, p. 253.

[15] Camus, *Lyrical and Critical Essays*, pp. 100–02.

ity of a fate that the speaker accepts, even though it is not what he would have chosen.[16]

Overall, his attitude is one of resignation: "Oh, if there's an original thought out there, I could use it right now." In Kierkegaard's *Fear and Trembling*, a pseudonymous author known as "Johannes de Silentio" distinguishes between two characters, the "knight of faith" and the "knight of infinite resignation." The former is a person who remains "true to his love" in a life that is united by an absurd faith, which constitutes "the highest passion in a human being."[17]

The knight of infinite resignation, on the other hand, is someone who has abandoned all hope but who does not forget whatever has been most precious in his life. He may not be in the mood to remember an experience of disenchantment, but he does—and, in trying to tie his memories together, he comes to understand how these real experiences weigh upon the present. Like the narrator in "Brownsville Girl," the knight of infinite resignation has renounced the passionate aspirations that oriented his life "before the stars were torn down," but he realizes that his present identity is largely defined by what he has cared about in the past, so that he would be a different person if he had not survived this particular disappointment.[18]

When, in the twentieth stanza of the song, we hear for the fourth time about a movie starring Gregory Peck, we realize that it serves as a point of reference for the speaker. By continually returning to a simple event around which so many emotions are organized, he reminds himself of who he is and where he has been. Even if he is somewhat the worse for the wear, he does not feel that all of his experience has come to nothing.

Oh Mercy: The Stage Sets Collapse

"There are no mistakes in life some people say," Dylan sings, adding: "It is true sometimes you can see it that way" ("Man in

---

[16] Nietzsche advocates *amor fati*, the loving embrace of necessity, in a number of places. See, for instance, *Ecce Homo* (New York: Penguin, 1992), pp. 37–38. On a fate which one has inherited and also chosen, see Heidegger, *Being and Time*, p. 351.

[17] Kierkegaard, *Fear and Trembling* (New York: Penguin, 1985), pp. 95, 143–46.

[18] See Kierkegaard, *Fear and Trembling*, pp. 72–73.

the Long Black Coat"). In other songs on the 1989 album *Oh Mercy*, however, we hear the voice of a narrator who has trouble seeing it that way. Instead of being reconciled to the way things have turned out, he is concerned about the fact that everything is broken. "Seems like every time you stop and turn around / Something else just hit the ground" ("Everything Is Broken"). It's not easy to harbor fond memories of everything that was most precious in life when all that remain are shattered fragments: indeed, there are "experiences which one cannot survive, after which one feels that there is no meaning left in anything."[19]

But the singer claims to be doing a pretty good job of dealing with his absurd situation—staying focused, keeping his feet on the ground—that is, most of the time. He understands what has happened, and says "I wouldn't change it if I could" ("Most of the Time"). Here, in the darkest song on the album, he makes it sound as if all of this misery, pain, and suffering can be traced to a frustrated love:

> Most of the time
> I'm strong enough not to hate
> I don't build up illusion 'til it makes me sick
> I ain't afraid of confusion, no matter how thick
> I can smile in the face of mankind
> Don't even remember what her lips felt like on mine
> Most of the time

The most he can claim is that he's "halfway content," that he doesn't "hide from the feelings that are buried inside," and that he doesn't even care if he ever sees her again—most of the time. Which means that, some of the time, he is less than halfway content, does hide from his feelings, and does care.[20]

Things might be easier for him if he could let it go, but like the knight of infinite resignation he feels that even though his love has come to grief, "he will never be able to wrench him-

---

[19] E.M. Cioran, *On the Heights of Despair* (Chicago: University of Chicago Press, 1992), p. 8. And see Simone Weil, *Gravity and Grace* (London: Routledge, 1963), p. 73.
[20] See also Ricks, *Dylan's Visions of Sin*, pp. 356–57.

self out of it," since he knows that "the content of his whole life lies in this love."[21]

And if he has become painfully aware of "the absence of any profound reason for living, the insane character of that daily agitation, and the uselessness of suffering," that is perhaps "the price that must be paid for the passions of this earth."[22]

By now it seems that the singer's mood of weariness threatens to consume everything: at one point on the 1990 album *Under the Red Sky*, he mutters, "You can have what's left of me" ("Born in Time"). Yet it sounds as if there is nothing left to give, and possibly nothing left to sing about anymore.

Further into the Absurd: *Time Out of Mind*

Just when you think he can't go on, though, he somehow manages to keep on going—which is fitting for an absurd hero or a knight of infinite resignation. Dylan's remarkable 1997 album *Time Out of Mind* begins in a familiar existential predicament, with a narrator "walking through streets that are dead," feeling sick of love but still "in the thick of it" ("Love Sick"). Skies are gray, and his mind is like a graveyard, but "that's how it is when things disintegrate" ("Can't Wait"). Then he adds a bit of black humor: "It's mighty funny, the end of time has just begun."[23]

Laughing sardonically at his condition may help him to resign himself to it, but his self-ridicule does not alleviate the sense of futility which is setting in like never before. "You broke a heart that loved you," he sings in "Tryin' to Get to Heaven," making what is both a wincing confession and a damning accusation. "When you think you've lost everything," he says later in the song, "you find out you can always lose a little more." Having learned this, he can only close his eyes and "wonder / If everything is as hollow as it seems."

---

[21] Kierkegaard, *Fear and Trembling*, pp. 70–71. For the knight of infinite resignation to give up his love just because it cannot be actualized "would be to lose the defining, stabilizing center of self and world." Edward Mooney, *Knights of Faith and Resignation* (Albany: SUNY Press, 1991), pp. 45–46.

[22] Camus, *Myth of Sisyphus*, pp. 6, 120.

[23] "When we laugh at a true absurdity," Ted Cohen suggests, "we simultaneously confess that we cannot make sense of it and that we accept it." *Jokes* (Chicago: University of Chicago Press, 1999), p. 41.

> I'm going down the river
> Down to New Orleans
> They tell me everything is gonna be all right
> But I don't know what "all right" even means

Where do you go from here, when you don't even know what would count as happiness? The poet feels as if he has been thrown into a world that he cannot understand, only for the sake of drifting or being driven toward some goal in which he does not even believe. Although he feels "almost like I don't exist," he is reminded of his existence by the suffering that he continues to undergo, which is a sign that he does still care ("Cold Irons Bound").[24]

However, in another song ("Not Dark Yet") he wonders if it will be possible to endure much more of this.

In the opening stanza of this raspy-voiced dirge, the singer introduces himself as steeled and scarred. Night is falling, "time is running away," and he cannot find a space in which to exist: "There's not even room enough to be anywhere / It's not dark yet, but it's getting there." What follows is a chronicle of the decline and fall of his ability to care about anything under the sun: "Well, my sense of humanity has gone down the drain / Behind every beautiful thing there's been some kind of pain." This is the voice of someone who has seen too much. Making a gesture of resignation, he shrugs his shoulders and says: "I just don't see why I should even care."

> I've been down on the bottom of a world full of lies
> I ain't looking for nothing in anyone's eyes
> Sometimes my burden is more than I can bear
> It's not dark yet, but it's getting there

The burden of existence may not always be too heavy to bear, but sometimes it is, and at this point the singer has simply had enough. He is anxious about the prospect of death, but he takes

---

[24] See Unamuno, *The Tragic Sense of Life*, p. 43. On "Cold Irons Bound," Dylan sings: "I found my world, found my world in you / But your love just hasn't proved true."

comfort in the thought of escaping from life altogether. In "Highlands," the sixteen and one-half minute anthem that ends the album, he sings: "I've got new eyes, everything looks far away." Although it certainly sounds as if he is finally opening himself to "the gentle indifference of the world,"[25] these are not quite the last words of the burnt-out dude walking off the face of the earth.

The Ends of Despair: From "Things Have Changed" to *"Love and Theft"*

That distinction is reserved for "Things Have Changed," which was released on a movie soundtrack in 2000, three years after *Time Out of Mind.* The song has been characterized as "a kind of farewell to every possibility for engagement in the world."[26]

Accompanied by driving rhythms, Dylan's voice (sounding increasingly like that of an old man) reports on a final passage into the absurd. "I'm locked in tight," he sings, but then he growls: "I'm out of range." When a rupture of such proportions has opened up between self and world, *things* lose their meaning because *I* no longer care. Hence the punch line: "I used to care, but things have changed."

Once again, Dylan's grim sense of humor shows up in the midst of an anguish that is dead serious: "Lot of water under the bridge, lot of other stuff too / Don't get up, gentlemen, I'm only passing through." In this world, there is nothing left to believe in or to hope for, and love exists only as a grotesque kind of desire: "All the truth in the world adds up to one big lie / I'm in love with a woman who don't even appeal to me." The lone note of hopefulness in this apocalyptic song is sounded when the singer makes reference to two characters who "jumped in the lake," then adds: "I'm not that eager to make a mistake." But even if he is not quite suicidal, he appears to have arrived at the nadir of existential desperation.

Nevertheless, life goes on, and so does the process of writing songs—even after what might have sounded like the writer's

---

[25] This phrase is used by the character Meursault in Camus's novel *The Stranger* (New York: Vintage, 1989), p. 122.

[26] Terrence Rafferty, "God is Dead. Bob Dylan Lives," *GQ* (June 2001), p. 102.

final words. On September 11th, 2001, Dylan released the album "*Love and Theft*," which takes up some of the existential themes of "Things Have Changed" in a number of places. Some of its lines might suggest that the singer has only wandered further into the absurd: "I say, 'How much you want for that?' I go into the store / The man says, 'Three dollars.' 'All right,' I say, 'Will you take four?'" ("Po' Boy").

If everything has lost its value, then why not just pay the four dollars and be done with it? However, it may be a mistake to interpret the lines in this cynical spirit, since the album also expresses a different perspective. The opening lines of "Sugar Baby" give voice to a transformed emotional outlook on the world: "I got my back to the sun 'cause the light is too intense / I can see what everybody in the world is up against." Rather than telling new stories of hope and disappointment, the poet is surveying things with an expanded sense of gratitude and compassion. The tragic sense of life is still most definitely present, but without the same agitated grasping. It is almost as if, by ceasing to expect anything at all from life, Dylan's narrator has opened himself to the possibility of seeing things in a different light. Even his romantic complaints reveal a change of tune: "I care so much for you—didn't think I could / I can't tell my heart that you're no good" ("Honest with Me"). Here, he acknowledges that he cannot bring himself to stop caring, even when faced with mixed evidence.

"Some of these memories you can learn to live with," he sings in "Sugar Baby," "and some of them you can't." There are times when "existence seems like some dirty trick," and it is always true that "happiness can come suddenly and leave just as quick." Yet, although life doesn't always seem to be worth living, he comprehensively accepts it, displaying an appreciation that could almost be called joyful. In "Mississippi," he claims that his heart "is not weary" despite all the debris of the shipwrecks he has experienced: in fact, "it's light and it's free / I've got nothing but affection for all those who've sailed with me." These words are not exactly bubbling over with jubilance, but they are more convincing as an existential affirmation for that reason— they do not require any kind of self-deception. And the person whose ability to care has been significantly diminished may be the one who is ready to love unselfishly, or "to give without taking hostages."[27]

This view is hinted at on earlier albums, but now it has assumed a new prominence: "There can be no love where feelings are denied, where one has not the courage to accept existence in all its facets, where one doesn't want to recognize pain."[28]

Love has "a way of tearing the world apart," as Dylan's narrator admits, but he adds that it is "not an evil thing" ("Sugar Baby"). This cannot be an observation; it must be a premise accepted on trust. Although the singer's voice has not lost its overtones of alienation, he seems to have a renewed belief in the possibility of love. Insofar as he does have this belief—since love, of course, also has a way of holding a world together—he begins to look more like a knight of faith.[29]

In another gesture of reconciliation, he makes peace with time: "So many things that we never will undo / I know you're sorry, I'm sorry too" ("Mississippi"). But, as if to insist that he is not wallowing in despair, he immediately launches into another line as the tempo of the music rises. "Some people will offer you their hand and some won't," and that's how it goes, but in saying this he reaffirms his acceptance of life in a world where the conditions of his own well-being are out of his control. Expressing a strange and beautiful faith, he sings: "I know that fortune is waiting to be kind / So give me your hand and say you'll be mine." His logic is this: chance events have been going horribly, so they must be due to turn around sometime. Here,

---

[27] Janet Gezari, "Bob Dylan and the Tone Behind the Language," *Southwest Review* 86 (2001), p. 488. Regarding the diminished ability to care, see the following lines from "Mississippi": "Got nothing for you, I had nothing before / Don't even have anything for myself anymore"; and "You can always come back, but you can't come back all the way."

[28] Aldo Carotenudo, *The Call of the Daimon: Love and Truth in the Writings of Franz Kafka* (Wilmette: Chiron, 1993), p. 106. This theme is discussed at greater length, in relation to Kierkegaard's writings, in my book *Wisdom in Love* (Notre Dame: University of Notre Dame Press, 2004).

[29] Kierkegaard, *Fear and Trembling*, pp. 75–79, 101. See also Mooney, *Knights of Faith and Resignation*, pp. 53–54. In *Youthful Writings*, Camus writes: "So many things are susceptible of being loved that surely no discouragement can be final" (New York: Marlowe, 1976), p. 206.

Dylan looks directly at a world lacking any clear purpose and makes an appeal that is filled with absurd faith in what is still possible. This is what may remain after a person has sounded out the depths of existential despair and come to terms with a finite and sometimes tragic life on the other side. In a universe from which all the stars have been torn down, a human being feels like a stranger. But it is not impossible to keep on living under such conditions, and Dylan shows us how it might be done. For this timely philosophical insight, we are forever in his debt.[30]

---

[30] I'm grateful to Jonathan Ellsworth and J.P. Rosensweig for many conversations on Dylan and philosophy, and to Jonathan and Sara Ellsworth for their hospitality while I was writing this in Santa Fe, New Mexico. My paper is dedicated to Sarah Pessin, along with the following line: "It's all so clear, I could never forget."

3

Who Killed Medgar Evers?

AVERY KOLERS

In his early song "Only a Pawn in Their Game," Bob Dylan argues that there are some people whom we shouldn't judge from a moral perspective. Being "pawns," they're incapable of moral choice—not the authors of their actions, but mere tools of others' agendas. Dylan makes this point in expressing a kind of contempt for Byron de la Beckwith, the white Southerner who fired the bullet that killed NAACP organizer Medgar Evers. Dylan would have us believe that even though Beckwith is "the one / That fired the gun"—his hand, eyes, and brain mere extensions of the bullet and handle—Beckwith "can't be blamed." Rather, there's a murder mystery here—who killed Medgar Evers? And rather than accuse Beckwith, Dylan appears to deny that Beckwith can be blamed.

Dylan's argument for denying Beckwith's agency in the killing is that the "poor white man" in the South is manipulated into race hatred by divide-and-rule tactics, his whiteness a cheap and easy "psychological wage" that keeps his anger directed away from his rulers and toward his black neighbors.[1]

---

[1] Pem Buck argues forcefully for a position like this in *Worked to the Bone: Race, Class, Power, and Privilege in Kentucky* (New York: Monthly Review Press, 2002). Mike Marqusee points out that Beckwith wasn't actually poor, so he wouldn't count as a pawn by Dylan's reasoning. The point, of course, stands for the general case, and I'll follow Dylan in using Beckwith as an example despite the incorrect application. See Mike Marqusee, *Chimes of Freedom* (New York: The New Press, 2003), p. 77.

"Only a Pawn" relates interestingly to other morally charged songs of the same period, including "The Lonesome Death of Hattie Carroll," where Dylan decries the lenient sentence handed down to a Maryland blueblood guilty of murder, and especially "Who Killed Davey Moore?" where Dylan deftly analyzes the moral responsibility of people in different institutional locations. In fact, I think a good case can be made that "Davey Moore" and "Only a Pawn" are companion pieces: the former asks the question, the latter answers it.

Over the course of this discussion we'll dip into some insights about moral responsibility that have exercised philosophers since Aristotle (384–322 B.C.E.). Aristotle connected knowledge, choice, and responsibility, arguing that people are morally responsible for their actions even when they act in ignorance or under duress.[2] But philosophers of the past century have complicated these connections by considering the role of factors we don't control—such as social relations and ideologies—in shaping our character, constraining our choices, and generating our worldview.

But more on this later: first I want to examine what "pawns" are, and how to recognize them among us.

What Is a Pawn?

Byron de la Beckwith could be a pawn only in a metaphorical sense. Literally, of course, a pawn is a chess piece, though in this case the literal is a fossilized metaphor: the word 'pawn' comes from the same root as peon or 'peasant', and denotes a humble foot-soldier. Pawns are the most numerous and least versatile chess pieces. Their expendability is a defining feature. They sit on the front line, protecting their more versatile, and hence more-valued, teammates. Pawns are unfree: except in their opening move, they may move only one space forward at a time; except when they take an opposing piece, they may move only straight ahead. For most of the game, *where they are*—blocking opposing pieces' path to the queen, say—is more important than *what they do*. Also, pawns start the game only six moves away from the far end of the board, where they may

---

[2] Aristotle, *Nicomachean Ethics* (Indianapolis: Hackett, 1985), Book III, Chapter 1, 1109b30–111b5.

be transformed into queens; but only in the rarest of cases does a pawn ever experience such social mobility.

Are there any human "pawns"? It depends which features are most salient. A pawn is most straightforwardly a piece in a board game—a mechanical plaything moved around by the whims of a transcendent agent. This form of pawnhood appears in Dylan's "gospel" era, particularly in songs like "Gotta Serve Somebody," where it suggests the Manichean struggle represented on a chessboard.

If this is what Dylan means in "Only a Pawn," then it follows trivially that Beckwith is a pawn, since *everyone* is a pawn. But this reading of the 1963 song seems incorrect because Dylan *denies* that everyone is a pawn: the fact that Medgar Evers's mourners "lowered him down as a king" when they buried him doesn't mean only that Evers was a different piece in a cosmic chess game, but rather that Evers is worthy of respect in a way that Beckwith isn't. Similarly, William Zanzinger, murderer of Hattie Carroll, is, if not a king, surely not a pawn—which is why Dylan thinks he deserves a harsher sentence. Pawns, Dylan suggests, are unfree in a way that other people are not. So pawnhood isn't about being God's plaything.

A pawn is on the front line of battle—the first to attack, and to die. This form of pawnhood accurately describes poor whites through much of American history, from the conquest and settlement of the West to the backlash against civil rights—not to mention the Civil War and the Vietnam War. But even if being on the front line is necessary for pawnhood, it isn't sufficient. Some people, such as freedom riders and those who desegregated lunch counters, volunteer for the front lines, and that's precisely why they're praiseworthy. So Beckwith's simply being on the front line is no reason not to blame him. The reason not to blame him is that:

> He's taught in his school
> From the start by the rule
> That the laws are with him
> To protect his white skin
> To keep up his hate
> So he never thinks straight
> 'Bout the shape that he's in

Dylan implies that the pawn is *duped,* or *brainwashed.* But by whom? Primarily the "South politician," who cynically uses "the Negro's name" to bolster his political career. But also the "deputy sheriffs, the soldiers, the governor": the castles, the knights, the queen.

Any time we suggest that someone is brainwashed, we'd better be prepared to explain how. Consider two relevant methods of brainwashing. In chess, pawns have the prospect of social mobility, of reaching the end of the board and becoming a queen. It's a vanishingly small option, but a real one that can be reached only by charging forward into battle. In the Apartheid South whites had a similar prospect—also vanishingly small—of social mobility. Added to this are the psychological wages of whiteness:

A South politician preaches to the poor white man
"You got more than the blacks, don't complain
You're better than them, you been born with white skin,"
   they explain

These small benefits distract poor whites from their real interests. Beckwith would be better off fighting *alongside* Evers; he would have to give up the deceptive wages of whiteness, but in their place he would earn the true wages of social equality.

To be a pawn, then, is to serve as a front-line defender of the powerful, putting yourself at risk because you incorrectly believe, due to indoctrination and illusory benefits, that you're defending your own interests.

Recognizing Pawns

The definition of pawnhood that's now on the table captures what Dylan means by calling Beckwith a pawn. But it doesn't provide empirically useful criteria for determining whether Beckwith—or anyone else, including you and me—really is a pawn. We need to translate our abstract notion into a testable one.

I want to suggest three conditions that are practically useful in determining who is a pawn and why, allowing us to assess Dylan's argument. First, a pawn shares at least one socially salient "objective" feature with both in-group (in this case, wealthy white men) and out-group (poor African Americans). "The poor white man" shares gender and race with the in-group, poverty and sometimes job description with the out-group. His in-group membership is therefore probationary, and so he risks being subordinated in much the same way as the out-group he in turn subordinates. A pawn is in what the philosopher Michele Moody-Adams calls a "liminal" position, a position between rigid social categories.[3]

Moody-Adams suggests that people in liminal positions are especially perceptive about contradictions and inequities in social structures, because they have, as it were, one foot in each group. But the second condition of pawnhood defeats this perception. The pawn's perceptive capacity is stunted or defeated by *shame*. The stigma of out-group membership is so strong, the desire to avoid it so intense, that instead of seeing more clearly, the pawn engages in outrageous displays of in-group membership. He is desperate to "never think straight"—or allow anyone else to do so, either—"'Bout the shape that he's in."

But these two conditions don't yet justify Dylan in treating pawns as beneath blame. To the contrary, they just provide a motive for murder. So what else must be true in order to conclude that someone is a pawn? The third condition I'll describe is actually compound—it's the combination of attacks on the knowledge, individuality, and clear-headedness of pawns.

First, the social stigma of out-group membership, and the pawn's shame at the prospect, must cause extreme duress that makes him desperate not to face his suppressed perception.[4] Maintaining his tenuous grip on in-group status must seem to be a matter of life and death—or perhaps more importantly, his in-group status must seem to him to mark the line between his life's having meaning or value, and lacking it.

Such desperation could result from the intensive bonding experience found in lynch-mob organizations like the Ku Klux Klan, which subsumes his identity and affirms his whiteness:

---

[3] Michele M. Moody-Adams, *Fieldwork in Familiar Places* (Cambridge, Massachusetts: Harvard University Press, 1997), p. 70.

[4] This puts the pawn in what Primo Levi calls a "gray zone." See Levi, *The Drowned and the Saved*, discussed in illuminating depth by Claudia Card in "Groping through Gray Zones," *On Feminist Ethics and Politics* (Lawrence: University of Kansas Press, 1999), pp. 3–26: p. 9.

And he's taught how to walk in a pack
Shoot in the back
With his fist in a clinch
To hang and to lynch
To hide 'neath the hood
To kill with no pain
Like a dog on a chain
He ain't got no name

The lynch mob shores up his in-group membership—whiteness is of the essence of the KKK—and gives his life meaning by subsuming his identity in a larger whole.

Second, the pawn may believe that he has not started the fight, that his society is sinking into a "state of nature" as Thomas Hobbes (1588–1679) imagined it: a "war of all against all." In such circumstances, joining the battle seems like the most natural thing in the world. Demanding of people that they refuse to take up arms when faced with a Hobbesian state of nature is perhaps too much to ask.

Of course, early 1960s America was many things, but it was no Hobbesian state of nature. To the contrary: hierarchies were rigid and opposition to them was largely peaceful. (Pretty much all the political violence occurred in *defense* of the hierarchies.) So it would seem dubious to exonerate Beckwith by appeal to a war of all against all.

But what's crucial isn't so much the fact of the matter as what Beckwith *believes* to be the fact of the matter. *Because* he has fallen in with a lynch-mob organization, Beckwith *believes* that things have come to a head and all responsible citizens have to choose a side and fight.

Such a situation may seem more improbable than it is. Widespread fears of some peril we face, and the supposedly necessary extreme solution to it, are disturbingly common. How many exaggerated threats—the domino theory, the "yellow peril," the "red menace," "reefer madness," the "crime wave"—have corralled citizens into fearful support of immoral policies? We may admire people who manage to keep their composure despite such intense propaganda, but it's less clear that those who fall for it are individually blameworthy.

Judging Pawns

Whether Dylan is right that Byron de la Beckwith "can't be blamed" for killing Medgar Evers seems to have become a matter of epistemology, of *knowledge*. Plainly, Beckwith did not know that his real enemies were the "South politician" and his ilk, rather than the NAACP. But *should* he have known these things? Can we hold him responsible for *not* knowing? In other words, given that he is ignorant of these things, is he *culpably* ignorant?

Culpable ignorance is a branch of negligence—failing to do something that you were supposed to do. But culpable ignorance is delicate because what you were supposed to do was to *know* something, and knowledge seems to be at the core of responsibility: how can you be expected to know that you should've known what you didn't know? We inevitably judge culpable ignorance from the standpoint of knowing whatever it was that the person in question didn't know, and this risks clouding our judgment about whether and how they could have known it. Inadequate sensitivity to the problems of knowledge—"Monday morning quarterbacking," "20/20 hindsight," and so forth—is itself a vice. So we must be careful. If we conclude that Beckwith is culpably ignorant, then he is morally blameworthy for his failure to know, and hence for killing Evers. Using Aristotle's terms, although Beckwith acts *in ignorance*, he is responsible for that ignorance, so he is responsible for the action.[5]

But if Beckwith faces the combination of forces Dylan describes—acute status anxiety and shame, indoctrination by a lynch-mob organization, and hence fear of a Hobbesian war of all against all—Beckwith may be *blamelessly* ignorant. Or again in Aristotle's terms, if Beckwith's action is *caused by* ignorance of the particular characteristics of his act—"what he is doing" or "the result for which he does it"—then the act is non-voluntary and he may *not* be responsible for his action.[6] On this interpretation, Beckwith is like a soldier who kills someone in a "friendly fire" incident. The soldier intends to kill an enemy, but is for

---

[5] *Nicomachean Ethics*, Book III, Chapter 1, 1110b25–31.
[6] *Nicomachean Ethics*, 1110b25–31.

some reason unable to determine which side his victim is on. Culpability depends on the reasons for the soldier's ignorance.

You might protest here. Surely Beckwith knows the particulars perfectly well: he's killing an NAACP organizer in order to defend Apartheid in the American South. There's no ignorance involved at all. Or so you might say. But there are particulars, and then there are particulars. Understanding an action requires particular knowledge not just of the physical features of the act but of its context. The context may make all the difference. As Dylan describes him, Beckwith fears civil rights as a threat to his community's existence and his life's meaning. He thinks race is a natural, biological, maybe even divinely ordained category. He thinks racial stratification is for the best. He thinks the "South politician," "the deputy sheriffs, the soldiers, the governors" are protectors of "the poor white man," not that he's "used in the hands of them all like a tool." Beckwith is so badly mistaken about the context that this error feeds back and makes him misunderstand the particulars. Beckwith knows the particulars, but misunderstands them because he has an incorrect *empirical theory* of the social world around him.

Aristotle would be unmoved: he holds people responsible even if they are ignorant of general principles. But Aristotle has in mind *moral* principles. What he doesn't consider are *empirical* general principles. These aren't the sorts of beliefs for which ordinary experiential evidence is available. They're empirical beliefs, but still theoretic beliefs.

The reason Beckwith has a hard time identifying which side his victim is on is that Beckwith is (we're assuming) poor and white in a white supremacist society, which imbues his life with an immoral meaning. Many philosophers would conclude from this that Beckwith is the victim of bad "moral luck."[7] Moral luck is *luck* because he can't do anything about it, but *moral* because it determines whether he's a morally good or bad person. It's a scary notion: by sheer chance, we could be immoral, or just have

---

[7] Allen Buchanan powerfully discusses his own moral luck in overcoming his pre-Civil Rights Southern white childhood. See "Political Liberalism and Social Epistemology," *Philosophy and Public Affairs* 32 (2004), pp. 95–130. This is a pretty big topic in ethics these days, set off initially by Bernard Williams's essay "Moral Luck," in his book *Moral Luck* (New York: Cambridge University Press, 1982).

a much harder time overcoming obstacles to moral behavior. If this is the case—if Beckwith is the victim of bad moral luck— then we have to hold him responsible for his crime but admit that in performing the crime he's a victim of a kind of chance.

But there's chance, and then there's chance. The bad luck of tripping on a tree root and spraining my ankle is just bad luck. But the bad luck of tripping on an unmaintained sidewalk and spraining my ankle is not *just* bad luck, it's bad luck that was predictable when the city reduced infrastructure funding. And the city deserves some blame for that. So too with Byron de la Beckwith's bad moral luck. The bad moral luck of being a poor white man in a white supremacist society is not *just* bad luck, it's bad luck that was predictable when white supremacy was instituted. More strongly, it's bad luck on which the survival of white supremacy relies.

The best reading of Dylan's argument in "Only a Pawn" may be that Beckwith's bad moral luck, while it doesn't fully exonerate him, reflects back on all white people, including Dylan himself and most of his audience.

The Mystery Solved

In "Who Killed Davey Moore?", Dylan presents a murder mystery, and proceeds to interrogate the suspects—the referee, the angry crowd, the manager, the gambling man, the boxing writer, and climactically, "the man whose fists / Laid him low in a cloud of mist":

> "I hit him, I hit him, yes, it's true
> But that's what I am paid to do
> Don't say 'murder,' don't say 'kill'
> It was destiny, it was God's will"

Each suspect pleads innocent and shifts blame. Mike Marqusee suggests that these protestations of innocence are in bad faith. The suspects, he writes, "condemn themselves out of their own mouths" with "all the routine rationalizations."[8]

---

[8] Marqusee, p. 72. Marqusee does note that Dylan "place[s] money at the center of boxing's ethical morass" (p. 73).

This seems to me half right. "Davey Moore" documents a murder mystery and interviews the suspects, but ends with the mystery unsolved—the last two lines, like the first, simply pose the question. And if the moral argument of "Only a Pawn" is correct, then the suspects in "Davey Moore" are not wrong to put at least some of the blame onto others.

"Only a Pawn" solves these two murder mysteries by recognizing that political crimes are best understood from a political perspective. From a political perspective, we adopt what the philosopher P.F. Strawson calls an "objective" attitude.[9] When I speak to you individually, I treat you as a responsible agent; I adopt "reactive attitudes" such as gratitude, blame, respect, or resentment towards you. I will blame you if you do something to hurt me, thank you if you help me. But when we analyze social phenomena—jobless claims, polling data, trends in KKK membership—we adopt objective attitudes, such as gladness or displeasure. I may be glad that jobless claims are down, but I won't be grateful, because the decline in jobless claims isn't an action anyone took in my behalf. Except in rare circumstances—say, I'm discussing my psychiatric condition—we don't, and can't, take objective attitudes toward ourselves. We have to treat ourselves as agents, not vectors.[10]

By giving voice to the suspects in "Davey Moore," Dylan forces us to adopt reactive attitudes. Their protestations that "you can't blame me at all" may be disingenuous, but they're right that no one person—even (or rather, *especially*) "the man whose fists / Laid him low in a cloud of mist"—bears all the blame for the boxer's death. By the end of the song the mystery remains unsolved.[11]

In contrast, Dylan solves the murder of Medgar Evers (and by analogy of Davey Moore) by giving Beckwith neither voice nor name. By adopting only objective attitudes towards him, Dylan makes Beckwith ineligible for praise and blame. When you're a

---

[9] P.F. Strawson, "Freedom and Resentment," *Proceedings of the British Academy* 48 (1962).

[10] Randy Newman plays with this fact in "Rednecks"—itself something of a response to "Only a Pawn."

[11] The political analysis in "Davey Moore" may seem obvious, in this context, but when I asked my Business Ethics students one semester who killed Davey Moore, remarkably few of them offered political analyses. Several said, "he killed himself."

pawn your body *moves*, but you don't *act*. Dylan doesn't distinguish between gun and man, interspersing them as he lists their
relevant parts—a bullet, a finger, a handle, a hand, two eyes,
and a brain. Beckwith is the weapon, not the murderer: a pawn,
not a player. And if Byron de la Beckwith is a pawn, then white
supremacy murdered Medgar Evers—and professional boxing
killed Davey Moore.

But this risks going too far. Even if we want to blame white
supremacy and professional boxing, we can hardly conclude
that *no* responsibility rests on the shoulders of "the one / That
fired the gun" or "the man whose fists / Laid him low in a cloud
of mist."

Here's where, I think, Dylan's argument is most subtle. Even
though the *verses* of "Only a Pawn" address Beckwith's moral
psychology, the *refrains*—the conclusions—are about *blame*.
Our *blaming behavior*—our decisions about whom to blame, for
what, and how—is up to us. These killings are political crimes,
and our blaming behavior is a political act.

What good would it do for a white man like Bob Dylan to
blame Byron de la Beckwith for this murder? White supremacy
manufactures Byron de la Beckwiths in industrial proportions,
because it depends on their lynch-mob services. Beckwith's
place in the white supremacist social structure is a matter of
moral luck. He does, to be sure, have some control over
whether he overcomes this indoctrination, but the duress and
poverty surely make it unsurprising that poor white men rarely
do so. But poor white men are not the only people caught up
in white supremacy: white people in general are as complicit in
Medgar Evers's murder as the "angry crowd" and the "gambling
man" are in the murder of Davey Moore. In the end, Dylan stops
just short of altogether denying that pawns are morally responsible. Instead, raising one eyebrow he casts a wary eye over at
the rest of us. If we plead innocence and shift blame onto Byron
de la Beckwith, we play right into the hands of the Southern
white elite by ignoring the bishop, the castle, and the knight, but
attacking the pawn.[12]

---

[12] I'm grateful to Craig Christopher, Karen Christopher, David Imbroscio, Eileen
John, Morgan Jones, Jason Kawall, Linette Lowe, Leigh Viner, Thad Williamson,
and the editors of this volume and series for comments and discussion.

4

Great White Wonder: The Morality of Bootlegging Bob

JAMES C. KLAGGE

In 1969 a blank white double album appeared on the shelves of a few record stores. Dubbed *The Great White Wonder*, presumably because it resembled the Beatles' *White Album* in appearance, in fact it was twenty-three previously unreleased recordings by Bob Dylan—approved by neither Dylan nor his record company. So began the musical bootlegging business: In the ensuing decades dozens more illicit albums, and then thousands more illicit compact discs, appeared with studio and concert recordings of Dylan and of many other musicians as well. But is there anything morally wrong with bootleg recordings?

Waddya Mean?

I define these terms
Quite clear, no doubt, somehow ("My Back Pages")

Questions like "Are bootleg recordings morally wrong?" provoked the first real philosopher in the Western tradition, Socrates (470–399 B.C.E.), to insist that people *define* the words they use before they tackle difficult questions. While this sometimes appeared to be hair-splitting to those he talked with, often it is important to know exactly what we are talking about. What is a "bootleg recording"?

Officials in the music and film industries often complain about how much money they lose from "bootlegged" movies and CDs, usually made in non-Western countries, and marketed throughout the world. They are cheap because no royalties go to the artists or the production companies, and because there are no quality controls.

Accounts in the media of these kinds of problems regularly use the words "piracy" and "bootlegging" interchangeably. But there are good reasons for having the two different words. Cheap, knock-off copies of already-available CDs and DVDs made without permission of the production company are "pirated" products. They take an artistic work that is available on the market and reproduce it at a much lower cost. The most familiar form of this kind of reproduction now is illegally downloaded music and movies, copied for free. Record and film companies estimate that they lose billions of dollars per year to this kind of pirate activity. But bootleg CDs are not pirated CDs. Bootleg CDs contain performances that are not commercially available, because either the artist or the production company has chosen not to make them available.

Pirates steal a product that is already available; bootleggers make a product available. The original bootleg was whiskey, which was sometimes hidden in the leg of a boot. Now the product is a musical performance. Secret recording equipment can also be hidden in the leg of a boot. Ironically, Sony, which owns Dylan's recording company Columbia Records, makes miniature digital tape recorders with "Stealth" microphones! These are a favorite with bootlegging concert-goers.

By far the most common bootleg recordings are live performances. The *Great White Wonder* album included just two live performances: "The Death of Emmett Till," from a radio broadcast in 1962, and "Living the Blues," from a television broadcast in 1969. But now thousands of Dylan's live concerts are recorded in their entirety and shared or sold in CD form. Also bootlegged are recordings that have been made either in the studio or in less formal circumstances but not used in official releases. *The Great White Wonder* included four unused recordings from the studio in 1963 and 1965, and the rest of the recordings were from home sessions in 1961 and 1967.

Distribution of bootleg music has varied through the years. Originally record albums, like *Great White Wonder*, were carried by some independent record stores. Sometimes they were kept behind the counter. The same has been true of bootleg CDs, which could be found in some independent record stores through the late 1990s. But because record companies threatened to withdraw their official releases from stores that carried unofficial releases, there was always a larger black market that operated by mail-order and at swap meets: "Even the swap meets around here are getting pretty corrupt" ("Brownsville Girl"). Now business is done primarily over the internet, which is harder to police. There has also been a gradual and now widespread shift from pressed CDs to burned CD-Rs.

Is This Stuff Any Good?

Some of these bootleggers, they make pretty good stuff
   ("Sugar Baby")

What, if any, value do bootleg recordings have? If they are worthless or of little value, then there would seem to be no justification for making them available. But if they are valuable, then that would provide an initial—*prime facie*—justification for bootlegs. In fact, they have considerable musical and historical value.

The main reason that bootleg music has a bad reputation is that most people imagine bootleg recordings to be poor quality. This is sometimes true, especially when the recordings are of concerts from the 1960s or 1970s made by audience members using cheap portable equipment. And some studio recordings are early, perhaps incomplete, run-throughs of songs, or alternate arrangements that were ultimately rejected.

But many recordings of concerts come from the soundboard, the way officially released concerts are recorded; and increasingly, portable recording equipment brought by audience members is so good that it is difficult to fault the quality of audience recordings. (Sony has seen to that.) And where early or alternate studio arrangements are concerned, value is truly in the ear of the beholder. Eventual official releases of early versions of "Forever Young" and "Every Grain of Sand" made quite clear not only the historic value but also the sheer musical value of some once-rejected versions.

Infamously, five tracks of *Blood on the Tracks*, recorded in New York City, were later rerecorded in Minneapolis and replaced on the ultimate release of the album—"Tangled Up in Blue," "Idiot Wind," "If You See Her, Say Hello," "You're a Big Girl Now," and "Lily, Rosemary, and the Jack of Hearts." The early New York versions had an intimacy and informality that led Dylan to replace them. Whether this was an improvement is a judgment call that many fans do not want to have made for them. Since then Columbia Records has released early versions of four of the five songs (not "Lily"), but only one of those four is actually the "test-pressing" take that was originally intended for release ("Big Girl").

Notable alternate versions from other occasions that have yet to be heard officially include "New Danville Girl" (a stripped down version of "Brownsville Girl"), an electric version of "Blind Willie McTell," two versions of "Visions of Johanna," and two versions of "Caribbean Wind." In the 1985 interview published in *Biograph*, Dylan said about "Caribbean Wind":

> That one I couldn't quite grasp what it was about after I finished it. Sometimes you'll write something to be very inspired, and you won't quite finish it for one reason or another. Then you'll go back and try to pick it up, and the inspiration is just gone. Either you get it all, and you can leave a few little pieces to fill in, or you're trying always to finish it off. Then it's a struggle. The inspiration's gone and you can't remember why you started it in the first place. Frustration sets in. I think there's four different sets of lyrics to this. Maybe I got it right, I don't know. I had to leave it. I just dropped it. Sometimes that happens.

In this case, the earlier versions were the more inspired, yet they remain unreleased.

Dylan's revisions of his songs have not been limited to the studio. Many of his songs have continued to grow and change in live performances. As Dylan said in the spoken introduction to "I Don't Believe You," on *Live 1966*: "It used to be like that. Now it goes like this." For fans who see concerts as an opportunity to hear favorite performers simply reproduce their greatest hits all in a row, these kinds of variations will seem at best uninteresting and at worst unfortunate. But for artists and fans who value growth and expression, the variations are the lifeblood of performance. This is the main reason that Dylan's concerts have been so thoroughly bootlegged.

The best-known example of this kind of growth is Dylan's electrified versions of songs in the 1965-1966 tour. The ongoing changes to "Tangled Up in Blue" have been documented on the officially released *Real Live*. And other fascinating examples are rearrangements of "A Hard Rain's A-Gonna Fall" for the 1981 tour, and even a performance with an orchestra in Japan in 1994. The fullness and pleasure of these arrangements give the song a very different meaning, more hopeful and less apocalyptic.

Dylan's live performances are often criticized for a lack of feeling. It has to be admitted that this is sometimes true, and his performances can be quite variable in this way (as his officially released live albums show). But on some occasions Dylan finds just the right feeling for a song, and this makes all the difference, sometimes making the performance vastly superior to the released version.

His Christian concerts in the fall of 1979 were noticeably more compassionate than judgmental, when compared to the studio renditions on *Slow Train Coming* and *Saved*. And unique live performances of "Abandoned Love" (in 1975) and "Caribbean Wind" (in 1980) simply come alive. In cases such as these the recordings fill us with wonder at Bob Dylan's grasp of life and his ability to convey it.

The fact that Dylan performs some hundred concerts a year, and has been doing so each year since 1988 on his "Never-Ending Tour," suggests that he cares deeply about performing. Even if he doesn't do it well every night, he manages impressive performances on a regular basis, performances that are witnessed by only a few thousand people at a time. If such performances were simply left to the memory of those who were there, it would be a great loss. But recordings miraculously capture these performances, and bootleg distribution allows us to (re)live them after all.

One of the most important events in the history of popular music was Dylan's decision to "go electric." While there were indications of this on his officially released album *Bringing It All Back Home*, and the single "Like a Rolling Stone," the impact was truly experienced at the Newport Folk Festival in July 1965. There Dylan and a pick-up band of electric blues musicians performed three songs—"Maggie's Farm," "Like a Rolling Stone," and "It Takes a Lot to Laugh, It Takes a Train to Cry." The crowd of mostly folk fans was quite provoked—many negatively. While most fans of rock music have heard the story told, they have yet to hear the actual performance and the reaction of the crowd. Few know that Dylan was then convinced to come back on stage to perform two more solo acoustic songs—"It's All Over Now, Baby Blue" and "Mr. Tambourine Man."

Understanding Dylan as a performer requires knowing how he can use the reactions of a crowd for his energy. The best example of this is the now-released *Live 1966* concert. But the Newport Folk Festival in 1965 and the Christian concerts of 1979 and 1980 are also important examples.

The most important value of bootlegs is that they provide us with new songs that have never been released—songs that are sometimes every bit as good as the best of Dylan's officially released work. Usually these overlooked songs came during times when Dylan was overflowing with musical ideas. From the early 1960s notable songs are "Dink's Song," "Long Ago, Far Away," "Long Time Gone," "Farewell," and "You've Been Hiding Too Long." From the 1967 period of the *Basement Tapes* there are "Sign on the Cross," "I'm Not There (1956)," "Silent Weekend," and "All You Have to Do is Dream." From the Christian period there are "Ain't No Man Righteous, No Not One," "Ain't Gonna Go to Hell for Anybody," "Cover Down, Break Through," "Thief on the Cross," "City of Gold," "Let's Keep It Between Us," and "Yonder Comes Sin."

So there is a strong case that unreleased recordings of some of Dylan's studio work and his live concerts have a great deal of value, both musically, for the pleasure and understanding of our humanity they give, and historically, for the understanding they convey about Bob Dylan as an artist and human being. These are the very things we value in art and music, and they are present in unreleased recordings as well as in officially released recordings.

Indeed, Dylan and Columbia Records recognize this fact. As a result, over the years they have released some recordings that remained unreleased for too long. The *Basement Tapes*, *Biograph*, and the *Bootleg Series* volumes are clear examples of this recognition. While fans of bootleg material buy all of these official releases, they also buy fuller and better versions that remain unreleased.

Whereas the *Basement Tapes* official release provides mono versions of sixteen songs recorded in 1967 by Dylan and the Band (the other eight are just the Band), bootleg releases provide four or five CDs worth of recordings from that summer, many in stereo. Though Columbia has tried to release four of the

New York recordings from the test-pressing that were left off the final *Blood on the Tracks*, they have used slightly different tracks in two cases, and with the release of the earlier "Idiot Wind" on the *Bootleg Series, Volumes 1–3* they left off the organ overdub, even though the booklet claims (p. 49) that you can hear it! In response to the official *Bootleg Series, Volumes 1–3*, bootleggers released three sets of 3 CDs. When Columbia released a complete concert on the *Bootleg Series, Volume 4: Live 1966*, bootleggers released an eight-CD set of all the soundboard recordings from that tour.

While Columbia Records has been responsive to calls for more releases, what we have seen is how much more there is to go, and how much better it can be done. There is little question that bootleg recordings have great value and deserve to be released.

But Is It Right?

Do you have any morals?
Do you have any point of view? ("Tell Me")

The production and sale of bootleg recordings is illegal. This has been emphasized by major arrests and convictions of bootleg manufacturers and distributors in March 1997 and July 2004.

But Dr. Martin Luther King Jr. (1929–1968) reminded us that there is a difference between "illegal" and "immoral." Something, such as segregation, can be legal and yet immoral. Or something like physician-assisted suicide might be illegal yet moral. What laws a country has in place can be an accurate reflection of sound moral judgments, or they can be in need of change: "Man's ego is inflated, his laws are outdated, they don't apply no more" ("Slow Train").

Let's look at the issues concerning whether bootlegs are immoral or not. The *prima facie* justification for bootleg recordings based on their value could be overturned if there were considerations that showed them to be wrong on other grounds. Some ancient philosophers who argued with Socrates, known as "Sophists," claimed that whether an action was right or wrong was just a *subjective* matter of whether it was in your own interests or not. Dylan reminds us of this idea when he says: "You know it's funny how some people just want to believe what's convenient" ("New Danville Girl," unreleased). There is, according to the Sophists, no *objective* right or wrong.

This attitude is one that many people hold. For example, people who illegally download music often think that it's okay, as long as they can get away with it. This is really just a way of holding that morality is irrelevant to our decisions. But such people are usually also confident in holding that terrorism and child abuse are wrong. Bob made a strong case, in his early recordings, that racism ("Death of Emmett Till," unreleased), classism ("The Lonesome Death of Hattie Carroll"), and militarism ("Masters of War") are wrong. Although it is harder to take morality seriously when it threatens to interfere with our own plans, we need to be consistent in our thinking. We need to take morality seriously.

Even if we do take morality seriously, we might think that behavior is moral if that's how everyone else behaves. Dylan is familiar with this attitude: "You say, 'Baby, everybody's doing it so I guess it can't be wrong'" ("Trouble in Mind," B-side single). Philosophers call this view *relativism*. Again, this can be a rationalization for illegally downloading music. But this was also what Dr. King's opponents believed. Certainly "everyone" believed segregation was okay—or at least many people did. But we know many people can be wrong. Many of Bob's songs ("I Believe in You," "License to Kill") remind us that a popular attitude can still be wrong.

So morality is not simply a matter of what everyone thinks. Morality requires us to examine what we are doing, not just how people view it. We need to look closely at some of the reasons that bootlegging might be considered wrong.

The most important argument against bootleg releases is the artist's *right* to control his material—what will be publicly released, and in what form. The theory of rights—in particular, rights to life, liberty, and property—was developed by the British philosopher John Locke (1632–1704), whose ideas influenced the American "Declaration of Independence." A performance is a piece of property, to be distributed at the artist's direction and with the artist's consent. As Dylan once lamented: "Everything that's happening to us seems like it's happening without our consent" ("New Danville Girl," unreleased). If bootlegging violates a performer's property rights, then it's wrong.

In theory this idea of property rights sounds plausible, but in practice things don't always work this way in the music business. There are a number of things that Dylan has planned to release, but couldn't. Columbia nixed "Talking John Birch Paranoid Blues" in 1962 and the original version of "Hurricane" in 1975 for legal reasons. There are concerts from Dylan's Christian period that he recorded and planned for release, but Columbia didn't think they would sell, so they weren't released. Dylan commented after a 1980 performance of the still unreleased "Ain't No Man Righteous (No Not One)": "I'm sure that's gonna be on our next album," but there was no such next album. There were recordings planned for the original four-CD version of the *Bootleg Series, Volumes 1–3* that had to be cut because Columbia decided a three-CD box set would be more profitable. Bootleggers circulate these things, presumably in conformity with Dylan's wishes.

More problematic is when bootleggers release material that an artist might not want released. However, this is already done by record companies. Columbia released *Dylan* in 1973, a collection of songs that Bob never approved for release—in fact a collection so bad that it has yet to be officially re-released in the U.S. in CD form. The point here is not that record companies are an adequate model for excusing the behavior of bootleggers, but that artistic property rights already function in a very contingent manner. While they exist, they are often in competition with other rights.

The abortion controversy is a good illustration of this competition. A pregnant woman may claim a right to control over her own body, but this has to be considered in the light of a possibly competing right to life of the fetus. Since rights can sometimes be *overridden*, we must make sure we know what all the relevant rights are. And then we must make judgments about which rights are more weighty.

Even if the simple right to property is not decisive, what about a right to privacy? At least an artist should be allowed a right to privacy. As Dylan once pleaded:

> There's some things not fit for human ears
> Some things don't need to be discussed
> Oh, darling, can we keep it between us? ("Let's Keep It
>   Between Us," unreleased)

If Dylan records songs that he feels are too personal, such as the New York versions of some of the *Blood on the Tracks* tracks, doesn't he have a right to withhold them?

Perhaps so. But it is surprising how little effect concerns about musical privacy ultimately have in artists' choices. The too-personal recordings from the New York sessions for *Blood on the Tracks* were eventually approved by Dylan for release. And such decisions seem to depend not on personal considerations, but on whether the record company thinks they can now be profitably marketed. Nearly all performers are now willing to include old demos and alternate cuts as additions to "remastered" re-releases of their old albums. It is hard to give much weight to artistic rights when integrity is so often up for sale in this way.

In any case, private recordings can only be circulated if bootleggers can get their hands on them. And they can get their hands on them only if Dylan allows other people to hear them. It's interesting that unissued studio recordings made in the last dozen years have not circulated in bootleg form. This is presumably because Dylan has now seen to it that his studio recordings don't fall into the wrong hands.

Finally, a right of privacy could apply only to studio or home recordings, not concerts—which are by far the main source of bootlegged material. Once someone performs a song in concert, it has already been shared, and a right to privacy has already been waived.

The rights of the performer and the recording company have to be balanced against any competing rights—perhaps those of the fans. If an artist had no audience, then there would be no countervailing claims. But artists have the ability to get their recordings distributed by record companies only because of their popularity with and support from fans—popularity and support that the artist sought.

Fans wanting increased access to music seems to constitute an important claim. Art is not necessarily simply private property. A performance is a piece of art at least partly in virtue of having a potential audience. To then insist that the audience has no say in access to the art is to undermine its status as art. Fans have rights too.

The issue of rights and access to art looks very different when the art is a physical object, such as a painting or a sculp-

ture, as compared to when the art is an electronically repro-
ducible performance. If a physical piece of art is owned by an
individual, then that puts severe limitations on public access.
Any possible rights of the public clearly conflict with those of
the owner, and presumably are overridden. But if an appreciation of a performance by one person, electronically, in no way
interferes with another's appreciation of it, it is hard to see why
ownership and control should be especially restrictive—as long
as proper royalties are paid.

Aren't They Ripping Him Off?

Do you want it for free? ("What Was It You Wanted?")

The main economic argument against bootlegging is that it
deprives artists and their record companies of huge amounts of
money, since bootleggers pay no royalties. However, most of
the estimates of losses—in the billions of dollars—are due to
piracy, rather than bootlegging. Music pirates clearly take sales
away from record companies. That is one reason it is important
to distinguish piracy from bootlegging.

It's hard to see how bootleg products deprive companies of
any money at all, since what is bootlegged is material that companies have chosen not to market. Usually, due to the large
scale of commercial record production, it would not be profitable for companies to market material that gets bootlegged,
since it would not sell enough.

Sales of typical bootleg CDs range from a few hundred to a
few thousand copies. (Now that burned CD-Rs are common, the
numbers can even be far smaller.) Best-selling bootlegs might
sell ten thousand copies. Bootleg producers operate in the
cracks that are unprofitable for record companies to exploit. A
given item would have to sell about fifty times as well as it does
on the bootleg market for it to be worth the attention of a record
company. Thus, record companies choose to forego the sales
that bootleggers make.

In fact, a case can be made that bootlegging boosts the sales
of record companies. It was because of the publicity that *Rolling
Stone Magazine* gave to the *Great White Wonder* bootleg album,
and the interest that it provoked in the public, that Columbia
Records eventually released the *Basement Tapes*. Dylan himself
was amused by the large sales of the official album because he

thought "everybody had it already." The same can be said for the on-going *Bootleg Series* releases by Columbia, and all manner of official releases from the vaults of record companies. In fact a search of "bootleg" on Amazon.com turns up literally scores of items being officially marketed with that label! Bootleg producers have not only catered to interest, but have created interest in unreleased material.

Once a recording sees official release, bootleg customers will buy it, and if it is well done, the market for the bootlegged version will dry up. (We have seen, however, that it is not always well done.)

Sony has done an impressive series of releases over the last few years of Pearl Jam concerts in minimal packaging, meant to imitate bootleg releases. (Though "minimal" is only a stereotype—some bootleg releases are lavish!) Perhaps the originator of this approach was Arista Records, which once sold CDs of Grateful Dead concerts—"Dick's Picks"—by mail-order.

Even if bootleggers inadvertently function as advance-marketers for record companies, they still need to pay royalties to artists for the use of their performances. In fact, some already do. One famous bootleg-producing company—Great Dane Records, in Italy—printed the following message on its releases:

> We bring to the attention of the performing artists . . . that upon publication of the present phonographic recording, the deposit of a sum for each copy made as fair consideration has been made on their behalf . . . [as required by Italian law].
>
> This deposit has been made in the form of a passbook savings account with the Banca Popolare di Milano . . . and will be transferred to the legitimate owners upon specific request.

While this may not be done by other companies, it should be. It would be interesting to know whether artists ever actually take the money. Presumably doing so would constitute acknowledgement of the legitimacy of the enterprise.

So, What's the Bottom Line?

Are you ready for the judgment? ("Pressing On")

We have examined some of the moral issues surrounding bootleg recordings, primarily in terms of conflicting rights: On the one hand, bootlegs may violate rights to property, privacy, and profits. On the other, they may support rights of fans. Some of these claimed rights turn out to be weak or problematic. On balance, bootlegs seem morally acceptable under the following conditions: Fair royalties must be paid. Laws against theft (of studio and soundboard tapes) must be obeyed. And perhaps, if one is impressed by concerns of privacy, only public performances should be distributed.

If bootlegs are morally acceptable with these provisions, then it is also worth wondering whether there are any legal changes that could be made to reflect the value and moral legitimacy of access to unreleased recordings. If the production and distribution of recordings within the limits mentioned above were legalized, presumably there would be an incentive for record companies to lease the use of recordings to smaller companies that would find the venture to be sufficiently profitable.

Reflecting on the value of Dylan's unreleased performances is essentially incomplete without hearing any of them. Perhaps the best the reader can do is listen to "Foot of Pride," "Angelina," and "Blind Willie McTell" on the *Bootleg Series, Volumes 1–3*, and recall that these songs were unreleased for eight years, and only released because bootleggers made them known. And then listen to the second, electric, disc on the *Bootleg Series, Volume 4: Live 1966*, and reflect that the performance went unreleased for thirty-two years. Even now, half the recordings on the *Great White Wonder* remain officially unreleased.

5

Just Like a Woman: Dylan, Authenticity, and the Second Sex

KEVIN KREIN and ABIGAIL LEVIN

From early in his career as an anti-war protest singer onwards, many of Bob Dylan's best-known lyrics tackle difficult political themes. Songs such as "Blowing in the Wind," "The Times They Are A-Changin'," "Hurricane," and "The Lonesome Death of Hattie Carroll" explicitly address issues of war, racism, and social injustice. Dylan's voice has served as a conscience to the collective soul of America—pointing out injustices we have committed and flaws in our worldview.

But any fan of Dylan will know that he has more to offer his listener than a nagging, critical, moral voice. Many of his best lyrics fall into a second category: personal songs of love and loss. "You're Gonna Make Me Lonesome When You Go," "Don't Think Twice, It's All Right," and "Lay, Lady, Lay" address universal themes, but of a personal, rather than political, nature. In these songs, Dylan is not acting as a moral conscience, but capturing experiences and expressing emotions that we are all (too?) familiar with. These songs present certain perspectives from which to view the realm of romantic relationships. They ring true for us and influence our understanding of our relationships and ourselves either by validating our feelings and experiences or by providing new ways to understand these aspects of our lives.

There is also a third category of Dylan song. Here, in some of Dylan's most famous songs, the political and the personal intersect. In songs such as "Queen Jane Approximately," "Like a Rolling Stone," "Just Like a Woman," and "To Ramona," Dylan offers critiques of individual attitudes toward materialism and social hierarchies. In these songs, Dylan's critique takes the form of presenting a flawed character who serves as a model of how not to act. If we take Dylan at all seriously as a social conscience, and many fans do, it is worth attempting to explicitly describe which qualities should be avoided and, according to Dylan, which of us are most likely to embody those qualities.

Why does Dylan launch this important discussion of contemporary vanity and materialism in lyrics that at first glance seem to be directed merely at selected women? Why risk burying this vital topic in lyrics that can be read only on the level of individual critique? We will see that there is clearly a more broad cultural critique at work in these lyrics—a critique of urban life in general—and we will see that Dylan attempts to seek shelter from the storm of shallow city life through women who have stayed outside of the culture he so clearly abhors. Women, then, play a complex role in Dylan's vision of the good life, and whether this vision is tenable—for Dylan, women, or the rest of us—is our topic in this chapter.

Dylan's Critique of Urban Materialism

As perhaps Dylan's best-known song, "Like a Rolling Stone" is an appropriate place to begin. The song addresses a woman who has fallen from a position of privilege. The song famously opens: "Once upon a time you dressed so fine / You threw the bums a dime in your prime, didn't you?" The suggestion here is that the female addressee held a high position in the social hierarchy, from which she behaved condescendingly towards others lower down the ladder. The idea that she has disregard for others who are lower in the social hierarchy is further developed in Dylan's remark that: "You never turned around to see the frowns on the jugglers and clowns / When they all come down and did tricks for you." This woman was clearly the center of attention, and used those around her for her own pleasure and entertainment. Further, Dylan seems to accuse the addressee of the song—and presumably others like her—of being not only callous towards others lower on the social ladder, but also guilty of the crime of wasting their own time:

Princess on the steeple and all the pretty people
They're drinkin', thinkin' that they got it made
Exchanging all kinds of precious gifts and things

Those at the top of the consumerist culture ladder fritter away
their lives by trading with each other the tokens of their success.
All of us who are familiar with this song will no doubt agree that
Dylan's bitterness at such societal workings are hard to overes-
timate.

Consider too the almost equally famous "Just Like a Woman."
Dylan again offers a scornful portrait of a woman who seems
caught in feelings of her own superiority, but spends more time,
in this song, on the emotional pain that must attend this way of
life. Here Dylan makes explicit a theme that was left implicit in
"Like a Rolling Stone"—the idea that at least part of what is
problematic with this lifestyle is its inauthenticity, or to use a
more colloquial phrase, its "phoniness." He writes:

Ev'rybody knows
That Baby's got new clothes
But lately I see her ribbons and her bows
Have fallen from her curls

In other words, while at first glance material possessions provide a façade of happiness, Dylan notices that, below the surface, they serve only to mask real pain. In order to find true
happiness, she needs to come to see that symbols of status do
not, in the end, establish her superiority:

Baby can't be blessed
Till she finally sees that she's like all the rest
With her fog, her amphetamine and her pearls

And, while she acts, in many ways, like a woman—taking, making love, aching, and faking—when it comes to real strength,
she is lacking, just like a little girl. Finally, the song's contrast
between the trappings of this brand of consumerist womanhood
and the fragility of girlhood ("But she breaks just like a little
girl") suggests that while possessions mask weakness, they don't
provide maturity, depth, or strength.

This theme of mistaking material and social gain as a path to true happiness is reiterated, albeit more compassionately, in "To Ramona," where Dylan seems to still care about the person underneath all of this materialism and social climbing. There he writes that:

> But it grieves my heart, love,
> To see you tryin' to be a part of
> A world that just don't exist
> It's all just a dream, babe
> A vacuum, a scheme, babe
> That sucks you into feelin' like this

Here the addressee is in real pain due to her mistaken world-view and priorities, which cannot help but arouse Dylan's compassion. Ramona is someone who has not experienced success in terms of social status or material wealth; one gets the feeling that she is on the outside of this world, trying to get in.

A further theme that emerges in "To Ramona" is the conformity that is required by this way of life, which presumably adds to its dissatisfaction. He writes:

> I can see that your head
> Has been twisted and fed
> By worthless foam from the mouth
> That hype you and type you
> Making you feel
> That you must be exactly like them

So we see that the problems that Dylan has identified in this line of songs constitute a broad criticism of those who participate in competitive social and material hierarchies: they are phony, conformist, shallow, and cruel. But how can we give an account of why one ought not to participate in them, especially when they seem to offer such enticing rewards?

Dylan and Existentialism: I Shall Be Free

In attempting to answer this question, it's worth pausing to compare Dylan's complaints and criticisms with those of the celebrated French existentialist philosopher Jean-Paul Sartre

(1905–1980). In a way that is to a degree analogous to Dylan, Sartre often took the role of a conscience to French society, criticizing what he saw as economic and social injustices. He also worked to clearly articulate both the nature of the human condition and how one might respond to it. Sartre argued that the fundamental claim of existentialists is that in the case of human beings "existence precedes essence." For all non-human objects in the world, Sartre claims, their qualities are, in a sense, given to them. Plants, physical objects, and animals do not choose what they are. Human beings, on the other hand, are distinguished by the fact that they are conscious and can decide for themselves how they will act. In making such decisions and following through in one's actions, human beings determine their essential nature for themselves. According to Sartre, one is not born a coward, hero, folk singer, or banker. If Dylan never learned to play a guitar and never wrote any songs, it would make little sense to call him a folk singer. One's actions, Sartre argues, determine what one essentially is.

Further, Sartre argues, whenever we choose an action, we cannot help but make the choice we would recommend for anyone else in our position—it would make little sense for a person to say that she would act in a particular way in some situation, but no one else who found herself in her position should do the same. Any good reason for one person to do something should be a good reason for anyone else to do likewise in the same situation. Thus, according to Sartre, when I make choices for myself, I am choosing for all of humanity— that is, I am making the choice that I think all humans, in my position, should make. Hence, we create our own nature, and, in a serious sense, according to Sartre, we cannot help but choose actions such that they determine what it is to be essentially human.

So, we are radically and entirely free, and hence, have no excuses for our actions, and our choices and actions constitute the essential nature of humanity. This is a very serious position to be in. It's a lot of responsibility to carry on one's shoulders. It is a standard existential point that to recognize and accept the freedom and responsibility of the human condition takes courage and strength. Sartre spent much of his life—through literature, philosophy, and social action—attempting to make people feel this sense of responsibility.

And here we can start bringing it all back home. Those who are honest, according to Sartre, will feel a sense of anguish at the awesome responsibility that accompanies acknowledging oneself as a conscious and free being. What about those who are not honest concerning this universal aspect of the human condition? Sartre claims that they deceive themselves or are in "bad faith" (*mauvaise foi*). That is, they deceive themselves about the human condition, their responsibility, and their motivations. Further, whenever one is dishonest with oneself, one cannot make consistent or well informed decisions and is, by Sartre's criteria, attempting to shirk one's responsibility as a free and conscious being.[1]

We are not claiming that Dylan would necessarily describe his view of the world and the people in it in these types of existentialist terms. Instead, we are suggesting that, on some level, he is getting at the same issues. It is our position that framing his critique in existentialist terms helps to bring these issues to light and is useful in explaining Dylan's criticisms of certain people and society in general. More specifically, we want to claim that what motivates Dylan's forceful criticism of the characters in the songs mentioned above is that they act in ways that betray their bad faith.

Dylan's Idealized Women: Her Hair Hanging Long

Just as a certain kind of woman seems to exemplify Dylan's discontent at a larger social pattern of consumption, so also a certain kind of woman harkens toward a possible resolution of this angst and a transcendence of that system. The kind of woman Dylan praises is personified in such songs as "Girl from the North Country," "Santa Fe," and "You're Gonna Make Me Lonesome When You Go," and the portrait he offers in these songs suggests a resolution to the crisis of vacuous consumer culture in images of a pre-industrial, pastoral archetype.

Dylan most often situates the locales of these idealized romances in pointedly non-urban spaces. His girl in "Girl from

---

[1] For Sartre's own, concise account of his position on these matters, see his 1946 lecture "Existentialism is a Humanism." For a longer and far more detailed account, see his *Being and Nothingness*.

the North Country," lives "where the winds hit heavy on the border-line." "Never Say Goodbye" opens with the lines:

> Twilight on the frozen lake
> North wind about to break
> On footprints on the snow

In "You're Gonna Make Me Lonesome When You Go," the scene is pastoral and idyllic:

> Flowers on the hillside, bloomin' crazy
> Crickets talkin' back and forth in rhyme
> Blue river runnin' slow and lazy

See "Time Passes Slowly" as well:

> Time passes slowly up here in the mountains
> We sit beside bridges and walk beside fountains
> Catch the wild fishes that float through the stream

More examples are easy to find. So, perhaps the first thing Ramona should do is take her cracked country lips back to where they came from. But, once she has done that, what kind of person should she be?

The answer is that she should try to be the type of person who blends in well with her rural settings. The imagery with which Dylan portrays women worthy of praise is, almost always, pastoral. In addition, the women are, almost without exception, innocent to the point of implausibility. The morally exemplary women in Dylan's songs almost invariably have long flowing hair, often decorated with flowers. In "Ballad in Plain D" Dylan relates: "I once loved a girl, her skin it was bronze / With the innocence of a lamb, she was gentle like a fawn." Consider as well "One More Cup of Coffee (Valley Below)":

> You've never learned to read or write
> There's no books upon your shelf
> And your pleasure knows no limits
> Your voice is like a meadowlark

Beyond these types of descriptions, Dylan gives little indication as to how the female characters in these songs spend their time, other than cooking for men, as we'll soon see.

Dylan's Interaction with Feminism

Dylan attempts to find authenticity, it seems, in women who have not been corrupted by the world of competitive social and material culture. Above, we framed the issue in the existentialist terms of Jean-Paul Sartre. However, on existentialist grounds as well, it can be argued that there is a serious problem with his solution. According to Sartre, human consciousness is constantly trying to transcend itself. That is, consciousness recognizes itself and is in a constant process of attempting to go beyond itself in its current state. This imperative to achieve transcendence follows from Sartre's understanding of what it means to be human—having the ability, through our choices, to define, and redefine, our selves. It seems to follow, then, that it is only insofar as we exercise this ability that we are truly acting as human. Thus, transcendence—as the exercise of this ability to redefine ourselves—is our fundamental humanity. As Sartre would have it, whenever Dylan writes a new song, or better yet, when he recreates himself in a different image, he transcends his current state. But what of the women in the songs above, the ones sitting in the cold north wind, or high in the mountains, or in the fields of flowers? They seem to be uncorrupted, but are they involved in achieving transcendence?

Simone de Beauvoir (1908–1986), Sartre's lifelong companion and fellow existentialist, would almost certainly have argued that the roles played by women praised in Dylan songs are not conducive to achieving transcendence. In one of the most influential feminist works ever written, *The Second Sex*, Beauvoir argues that, in their subjugation to men, women have been prevented from engaging in transcendent activities. Following Beauvoir, it seems that by praising only women who remain in traditional roles, Dylan limits the opportunities for transcendence available to women. For a very clear example, see "Sweetheart Like You," in which Dylan advises:

You know, a woman like you should be at home
That's where you belong

Watching out for someone who loves you true
Who would never do you wrong

Other examples abound in Dylan's work, some of which we've canvassed already.

Beauvoir's thought may also explain some of Dylan's reasons for being so upset at the less traditional women seen in songs such as "Like a Rolling Stone." The women he praises are almost all ones who have given him shelter from the storm, who are there to allow him to go someplace that is innocent and in which he can escape from the harsh realities of a competitive social world that contains deceit and injustice. But they can do that only by completely removing themselves from the modern world. The way Dylan describes them, the most active thing they do is grow their hair. Beauvoir complains of such women that, "The curse that is upon woman as vassal consists, as we have seen, in the fact that she is not permitted to do anything; so she persists in the vain pursuit of her true being through narcissism, love, or religion."[2] Of course, Dylan feels safe and relaxed in the company of women who do little else but lay across his big brass bed.

On the other hand, Beauvoir claims for any woman that:

> When she is productive, active, she regains her transcendence; in her projects she concretely affirms her status as subject; in connection with the aims she pursues, with the money and the rights she is in possession of, she makes trial of and senses her responsibility.[3]

Such women, active women, are pointedly not praised by Dylan. One might object that the women Dylan depicts in songs such as "Like a Rolling Stone," "Queen Jane Approximately," and "Just Like a Woman" are not criticized because they are women abandoning traditional roles, but because of the flaws in their characters. While this may be true, it seems peculiar that Dylan consistently launches his critique of these flaws through the bodies and lives of women in particular, and that the only women who escape this critique and are praised in his songs are those who are pastorally passive. One way to understand why

---

[2] Simone de Beauvoir, *The Second Sex* (New York: Vintage, 1989), p. 679.
[3] de Beauvoir, p. 679.

Dylan's vitriol at materialism seems directed at women in particular can be found through investigating some feminist critiques of women's traditional roles.

Dylan's Utopian Visions: Shelter from the Storm

Why would Dylan, who is so progressive and liberal in many other areas of his work, particularly in his anti-war and social justice songs, take this retrograde view of women as nurturers confined to the home in what is no doubt a man's world? One way of rescuing Dylan from the charge of essentialism[4] may be found in thinking of his view in this pastoral line of songs as utopian. Dylan, as a man, must dwell in the public sphere, which at the time when philosophers like Hegel or Aristotle were writing was an exciting and rewarding place to be. Dylan, however, with good reason, views the world of politics and public life as numbingly disheartening and corrupt. The debacles of Vietnam and Watergate, the assassination of Martin Luther King, and all of the other well-known political clashes of the sixties and seventies may be responsible for Dylan's and many other members of the dissenting counterculture's attempts to fantasize a way out. That the way out is envisioned as a simple, pastoral scene, where Dylan is in love with women who are uncorrupted by the public sphere by virtue of not having been exposed to it makes sense, given Dylan's situation of witnessing the public sphere of cities and politics at its most debased. Similarly, this may hold the key to finally understanding why Dylan's anger at consumerism is conflated with anger at women in particular. If Dylan, with most Western philosophers, sees women as outside of the public sphere, where consumerism takes place, then the sight of women who have fallen prey to its evils would be most devastating, in that it marks consumerism's march into every nook and cranny of life, even the most protected private sphere.

Susan Buck-Morss, a prominent contemporary interpreter of the social theorist and philosopher Walter Benjamin, suggests in her recent book *Dreamworld and Catastrophe*[5] that:

---

[4] Essentialism is the name given to a discussion which reduces the topic at hand to its biological, or innate, components.

[5] Susan Buck-Morss, *Dreamworld and Catastrophe* (Cambridge, Massachusetts: MIT Press, 2000).

The construction of mass utopia was the dream of the twentieth century. It was the driving ideological force of industrial modernization in both its capitalist and socialist forms. The dream was itself an immense material power that transformed the natural world, investing industrially produced objects and built environments with collective, political desire . . . As the century closes, the dream is being left behind. Industrial production has not itself abated . . . Consumerism, far from on the wane, has penetrated the last socialist bastion of mainland China to become, arguably, the first global ideological form . . . But the mass-democratic myth of industrial modernity—the belief that the industrial reshaping of the world is capable of bringing about the good society by providing material happiness for the masses—has been profoundly challenged.[6]

The death of this dream of collective or mass happiness as achievable through mass production and consumption is the death of one very powerful utopia, or "dreamworld," a term which Buck-Morss borrows from Benjamin to distinguish distinctly modern social myths from premodern mythology:

Whereas myths in premodern culture enforced tradition by justifying the necessity of social constraints, the dreamworlds of modernity—political, cultural, economic—are expressions of a utopian desire for social arrangements that transcend existing forms. But dreamworlds become dangerous when their enormous energy is used instrumentally by structures of power, mobilized as an instrument of force that turns against the very masses who are supposed to benefit. And in fact, the most inspiring mass-utopian projects—mass sovereignty, mass production, mass culture—have left a history of disasters in their wake . . . The dream of industrial abundance has enabled the construction of global systems that exploit both human labor and natural environments.[7]

What can we make of this idea of utopian dreamworlds in terms of understanding Dylan's critique of consumerism and his solutions to it? We want to suggest that we can view Dylan as an early seer of the corruption and eventual demise of the mass-utopian dreamworld of industrial production, and its corollary of a consumerist lifestyle. His songs critiquing women who have yet to see the catastrophic end to the dream that he sees are

---

[6] Buck-Morss, preface, i.
[7] Buck-Morss, xi.

meant as stern warnings that this dreamworld is no longer utopian in its promise of a better future, but instead has become corrupted by the "structures of power" that Buck-Morss and Benjamin warn against.

That said, the temptation to continue thinking in terms of mass utopia is deeply held, and as Buck-Morss and Benjamin note, revolutionary, in that it promises us a genuinely happier future, rather than merely treating existing oppressive structures as if they are tangible. Thus, we can view Dylan's pastoral utopias as an attempt to retain the good in utopian dreamworlds through eliminating the urban, public sphere corruption of the dominant dreamworld and replacing it with scenes that have yet to be corrupted. Thinking about these themes—the critique of consumerism, pastoral utopia, and women's roles—yields the insight that Dylan, caught up in the public/private gendered division of labor at a time when the public sphere was particularly disenchanting, longed to get out of this division—"I need a dump-truck mama to unload my head" ("From a Buick 6")—and retain that which is pure and uncorrupted by oppressive ideology. Thus the songs that offer a critique of the false promise of consumerism as happiness, and the songs that attempt to replace it with a new promise of purity and love in the natural world can be seen as part of an attempt to create a new liberatory dreamworld in the face of the collapse of the old one.

Sick of Love?

We wonder, in the more than four decades of Dylan's illustrious career, whether he still holds out the dream of a utopia of natural innocent love, salvaged from a world gone wrong? Dylan seems never to be able to stay for too long in the utopia he has created, always returning to the corrupted public sphere. Does he continue this equivocation, or does he eventually opt for one world or the other? One answer might be found in Dylan's recent Victoria's Secret TV advertisements, where he sings his recent hit "I'm Sick of Love" while women in lingerie slowly glide around him. While we would not want to read too much into a short televised ad, if we take it and the lyrics literally, not much seems idealistic here.

As an aging pop icon, sick of love and no longer seeking pastoral utopias, what is left but to be surrounded by scantily clad women while doing what he does best? Such a pastime certainly has its merits, but we have to wonder how those merits stack up to the idealistic expectations Dylan often seems to have had in such songs as "The Times They Are A-Changin'." Were they a-changin' into disillusionment with lingerie? Given the problematic nature of the public-private distinction for women's liberation, and Dylan's reliance on it, we should ask whether or not the folk singer who has been the collective conscience of our culture on issues of foreign and domestic policy should have that same role with respect to gender and relationships.

6

"Far Between Sundown's Finish An' Midnight's Broken Toll": Enlightenment and Postmodernism in Dylan's Social Criticism

JORDY ROCHELEAU

When Bob Dylan started singing that the times were a-changin' in 1964, he expressed the hopes of a generation of social critics for a freer and more just society. Dylan's analysis of racism, poverty, militarism, and repression brought social content into popular music previously dominated by banal professions of love. Yet Dylan quickly backed away from the role of progressive spokesperson. After the early 1960s, his work emphasizes uncertainties and ambiguities in understanding society and skepticism regarding all ideals. Dylan was booed at folk concerts after the mid-sixties not only for going electric but also for featuring music with ambiguous political content. His trajectory from social critic to skeptical individualist has been compared to that of his own sixties generation. But it is also a transformation that provides an instructive lesson in the history of political thought.

Dylan's protest music, which led to his being embraced as revolutionary spokesperson, exhibits Enlightenment social philosophy, while his work since this period provides an introduction to the political insights and ambiguities of postmodernism.

Enlightenment, Progress, and Courts that Are on the Level

The quintessential Enlightenment philosopher, the eighteenth-century German Immanuel Kant, defined enlightenment as "man's emergence from his self-imposed slumber." He called on humanity to use its reason to continually improve itself, expanding freedom and securing happiness. For Kant this meant not only using science and technology to master nature but also employing moral reasoning to organize society in a just manner. Kant argued for equality of treatment on the grounds that rational rules must be the same for all. He was an early proponent of the ideal of autonomy, the notion that individuals ought to live according to the light of their own reason. He held that public democratic debate would lead to social principles and institutions that preserved freedom and prosperity. Like all Enlightenment social philosophers, Kant believed human reflection and social action could overcome traditions and power structures that undermine freedom, equality, peace, and happiness. Kant realized that we are far from these ideals but that we have the ability to understand injustice and make progress.

Dylan's early protest songs charge that American institutions fail to live up to their stated Enlightenment ideal of equality. This is graphically portrayed in "The Lonesome Death of Hattie Carroll," in which the aftermath of the murder of a poor maid, Carroll, by the wealthy William Zanzinger is described. Dylan initially asks the audience not to cry over the hardship of Carroll, the privileges of Zanzinger, or the brutality of the crime. At the end of the song, Dylan takes us to the murderer's trial, where supposedly we can trust:

> that all's equal and that the courts are on the level
> And that the strings in the books ain't pulled and persuaded
> And that even the nobles get properly handled

Yet, justice is not done, as the judge hands Zanzinger "a six month sentence." By declaring that "now's the time" for our tears, Dylan is protesting legal discrimination and the influence of money and privilege on the law as unjust. He frequently returns to the theme of the United States' failure to retain equality before the law and to protect the rights of African Americans in particular. In "The Death of Emmett Till" he chronicles the murder of the African American youth from Chicago while visiting Mississippi. Ten years later, Dylan takes up another famous case of legal discrimination, that of the boxer Rubin Carter, falsely convicted of murder:

To see him obviously framed
Couldn't help but make me feel ashamed to live in a land
Where justice is a game ("Hurricane")

Dylan is aware that strong forces oppose the progress he recommends, yet, like Kant, he asserts that moral reflection ultimately shows the right path: "If you can't speak out against this
kind of thing, a crime that's so unjust / Your eyes are filled with
dead men's dirt, your mind is filled with dust" ("The Death of
Emmett Till").

Wanting Everyone to Be Free: Dylan's Chimes of Freedom

Although the racial caste system was Dylan's foremost target, he
was also concerned with economic inequality. "Ballad of Hollis
Brown" shines a light on poverty, when hunger leads a farmer
to kill his family and himself. While Dylan does not explicitly
decry injustice, the song points to those left out in a market
economy. It also points to the inhumanity of a society that provides shotgun shells but not sustenance. Dylan does not specify
what economic justice would involve—a right to employment, a
minimum income, or a fully socialized economic system.
However, he appeals to a universal judgment that poverty is
inhumane and that society ought to act to prevent it.

Dylan extols freedom as well as equality. Inequality itself
undermines freedom. To be discriminated against, much less
killed with impunity, denies an individual the right to live
according to the light of her own reason. When poverty and
economic necessity drive life, one lacks autonomy. In "North
Country Blues" Dylan depicts a woman whose life is dominated
by the iron mining business. After the mines have already taken
several family members, they suddenly close, leaving her in
poverty with a disintegrating community. While the company is
free to relocate to South America, market forces determine the
fate of workers' lives.

Dylan also cries out for social liberty to think and act without censure. Like Enlightenment liberal John Stuart Mill, Dylan
fears a tyranny of the majority that restrains individual development. Although "everybody wants you / To be just like them,"
Dylan insists on being "just like I am" ("Maggie's Farm"). Nor

does he desire freedom only for himself. Dylan would toll bells of freedom for "the outcast, burnin' constantly at stake" ("Chimes of Freedom"). Dylan protests a culture of intolerance—those who'll stone you for any misdemeanor, the "Idiot Wind" of gossip, and "[o]ld lady judges" who "dare / To push fake morals, insult and stare" ("It's Alright, Ma (I'm Only Bleeding)")—as much as legal restrictions on freedom. Dylan's defense of the unconventional and unpopular against repression displays his overarching commitment to autonomy.

Postmodernism: Questioning Reason and Progress

Postmodern political philosophy begins with a rejection of the Enlightenment belief in universal truths and values that can serve as the basis for social criticism and progress. Jean Francois Lyotard defines postmodernism as "incredulity toward metanarratives," that is, a refusal to accept that there are terms by which social progress can be understood and instituted.[1]

Dylan's turn away from protest can be seen as postmodern. This trend in his work begins with the appropriately titled album, *Another Side of Bob Dylan*, released in 1964 shortly after *The Times They Are A-Changin'*. The former focuses more on personal relationships and less on politics than Dylan's first three albums, with hits including "All I Really Want to Do" and "It Ain't Me Babe." The album also features "My Back Pages," an explicit repudiation of previously held social and political ideals. Dylan suddenly expresses skepticism about the meaning and desirability of the principle of equality:

> "Equality," I spoke the word
> As if a wedding vow
> Ah, but I was so much older then
> I'm younger than that now

The chorus implies that the ideal of equality was naive and did not constitute the clear and unambiguous path of progress that Dylan had thought. The song as a whole, and the last stanza in

---

[1] Jean-François Lyotard, *The Postmodern Condition* (Minneapolis: University of Minnesota Press, 1988).

particular, questions whether one can give any clear sense to terms like right and wrong and progress:

> Good and bad, I define these terms
> Quite clear, no doubt, somehow
> Ah, but I was so much older then
> I'm younger than that now

Many philosophers have questioned, like Dylan, whether and how social critics can gain a trustworthy perspective from which to critique society. If ordinary thinking is biased by personal interests and prejudice, constructed by contemporary culture and institutions, are critics' judgments not similarly biased? If all truths are relative to the perspective of the individuals who conceive them and are conditioned by cultural beliefs, it is impossible to judge in which direction progress lies. Perhaps even the ideals of equality, freedom, and democracy are just local values and not indisputably valid.

There's Too Much Confusion: Postmodern Ambiguity

Furthermore, even if in some sense equality and freedom were universally thought to be good, perhaps they are too vague to provide meaningful direction. For example, one might wonder what equality can mean when individuals have different skills and opportunities. Is formal legal equality, with "equality in school," sufficient? After thousands of years of dispute, political philosophers have reached no agreement on the meaning of equality, much less justice. If these ideals have no clear, unambiguous meaning, then perhaps they cannot be referred to as a source of enlightenment.

The limits of reason is a central theme in the work of Jacques Derrida (1930–2004), who argued that, contrary to Enlightenment thought, we can never gain unambiguous understanding of ideas. We think we have a clear idea of terms like freedom and equality, but each actually depends on other ideas that are unstated and not fully explained. Derrida avers that meaning and truth are always "deferred," never purely present in the ideas that we state. As he puts it, "The signified concept," the meaning of an idea, "is never present in and of itself, in a sufficient presence that would refer only to itself. Essentially and lawfully every concept is inscribed in a chain or in a system within which it refers to the other."[2] That is, our ideas only get meaning in relation to other concepts, even though these are not explicitly being thought of. Thus, we never have a complete grasp of the ideas we are talking and writing about. Since definitive understanding is always elusive, the project of reasoning together to reach a shared sense of justice, which preserves the freedom of all parties, is doomed.

Dylan, who is of the same generation as Lyotard and Derrida, shares the French philosophers' skepticism about rational understanding. Despite being well read, the modern Mr. Jones cannot figure out what is happening. He doesn't know who he is or what belongs to him, and he feels lost in a world of sword swallowers, one-eyed midgets, and geeks. Incomprehensibility may be the dominant theme of Dylan's post-protest period. Insurance men bring down kerosene from castles ("Desolation Row"), city fathers are "trying to endorse the reincarnation of Paul Revere's horse" ("Tombstone Blues"), and railroad men drink up one's blood like wine when they aren't smoking one's eyelids and punching one's cigarettes ("Stuck Inside of Mobile with the Memphis Blues Again"). The individual becomes lost in a baffling society and suffers seemingly meaningless violence.

Nor do the institutions of religion, education, and politics offer anything but confused and corrupt direction. "[P]reachers preach of evil fates" and "[t]eachers teach that knowledge waits" ("It's Alright, Ma (I'm Only Bleeding)"). Politicians are corrupt, self-serving, and ineffectual. One brandishes firearms while handing out free tickets to his son's wedding ("Stuck Inside of Mobile with the Memphis Blues Again") while in "I Want You" a drunken one "leaps upon the street where mothers weep." Desolation row gets no help from its blind commissioner, who they've got "in a trance" with "[o]ne hand tied to the tight-rope walker / The other . . . in his pants" ("Desolation Row"). Quick destruction or simple base gratification would seem to be the only options. The icons of Western reason and culture are made to appear ridiculous, or perhaps, all used up. Shakespeare is in the alley talking to a French girl ("Stuck Inside of Mobile with

---

[2] Jacques Derrida, "Différance," in *Margins of Philosophy* (Chicago: University of Chicago Press, 1982), pp. 3–4.

the Memphis Blues Again"), Einstein is disguised as Robin Hood
("Desolation Row"), Mona Lisa has the highway blues ("Visions
of Johanna"), Galileo's math book is tossed at Delilah
("Tombstone Blues"), and Ezra Pound and T.S. Elliot resolve
their differences with violence ("Desolation Row").

As Dylan's career continues, the calling into question of the
Enlightenment's view of reason becomes more pronounced.
Rather than simply usurping its ideals he offers an alternative—
and darker—picture of the world. One Enlightenment dogma is
that human reason will lead to progress and the gradual
improvement of mankind. Dylan calls into question the very
nature of progress, declaring that an apparent achievement of
the human mind such as the moon landing in fact sows the
seeds of our destruction: "man has invented his doom / First
step was touching the moon ("License to Kill"). Far from gradu-
ally improving, "the world is ruled by violence" ("Union
Sundown"). This pessimistic view carries over to human nature.
Whereas the Enlightenment generally offers an optimistic picture of man, Dylan declares that "[m]an's ego is inflated, his laws
outdated, they don't apply anymore" ("Slow Train") and that
"every man's conscience is vile and depraved" ("Man in the
Long Black Coat"). Perhaps the height of Dylan's skepticism
towards human reason comes in the so-called Christian period
with such lines as "[y]a either got faith or ya got unbelief and
there ain't no neutral ground ("Precious Angel"). Here, reason is
completely absent from the picture. The Enlightenment notion
of reason as authoritative—for Kant reason was able to lead us
to moral truth independent of God—is overthrown. By contrast
for Dylan, "there's only one authority / And that's the authority
on high ("Gonna Change My Way of Thinking"). While Dylan's
assertion of biblical absolutism could be argued to be pre-mod-
ern rather than postmodern, his dogmatic faith is tied to a similar skepticism regarding reason's power to better the human
condition.

Protest as Just More Propaganda

Dylan is critical of Enlightenment commitments not only
because of their uncertainty but also because ideals of progress
can undermine rather than further freedom. "My Back Pages"
implies that the progressive Dylan erred in "[f]earing not that

[he]'d become [his] enemy / In the instant that [he] preach[ed]."
Postmodernists such as Michel Foucault (1926–1984) have
argued that modern reason, with its ideals of freedom, justice,
and prosperity, takes away freedom even as it purports to further it. Foucault argues that knowledge is always linked to
power. His point is not that knowledge gives power to do things
to those who have it, as is meant in the common expression
"knowledge is power," but that what counts as knowledge is
determined by those who have power, and that knowledge itself
functions as a kind of power that dominates both its objects and
the subjects who possess the knowledge. For example,
Foucault's *Madness and Civilization* argues that rather than
identifying pre-existing mental illness, psychology creates insanity through its definitions and practices of separating the insane
from the sane. Rather than simply treating insanity, psychology
creates ideas of normal behavior and strategies for its cultivation
that control both the insane and the sane. "The asylum," writes
Foucault, "becomes . . . an instrument of moral uniformity and
social denunciation."[3] Knowledge leads to greater social control
rather than freedom. Moral and political understanding is no different. Concepts of goodness and duty control how we are sup
posed to understand ourselves.

Dylan's work from the mid-1960s to the mid-1970s, generally
considered his most original, depicts his ambivalence regarding
ideals, including freedom. For example, the haunting "It's
Alright, Ma (I'm Only Bleeding)" is a vivid expression of paths
to freedom as traps. That which is desired turns out to be only
false advertising, the fetish of consumers accustomed to material acquisition. Though freedom is continually promised, one is
trapped in its pursuit:

> Advertising signs they con
> You into thinking you're the one
> That can do what's never been done
> That can win what's never been won
> Meantime life outside goes on
> All around you

---

[3] Michel Foucault, *Madness and Civilization*, included in Paul Rabinow, ed.,
The Foucault Reader, (New York Pantheon, 1984), p. 149.

Dylan, like Foucault, became disillusioned with progressive movements. Socialism, rather than providing individual freedom and equality, became a new form of domination. Social movements demand obedience and purity in observance of the party line. Like religious zealots and military conscripts, progressives are expected to retain rigid discipline and blind obedience in their commitment to the cause. As Dylan sings, "some on principles baptized / To strict party platform ties" (It's Alright, Ma (I'm Only Bleeding)").

In addition to sensitivity to authoritarian tendencies in social movements and ideals, Dylan displays suspicion that protest itself is controlled by the system that it rebels against: "one who sings with his tongue on fire / Gargles in the rat race choir" (It's Alright, Ma (I'm Only Bleeding)"). By attempting to struggle, get ahead, be free, and grasp what is true and good, the singer and critic merely perpetuates the social system. It is not just that social forces tend to work against Enlightenment-type ideals, but that the ideals have become self-refuting.

Dylan's skepticism about the ability of any ideals and institutions to give us freedom continues in his work in the eighties. The 1989 album *Oh Mercy* finds Dylan exasperated that "[w]e live in a political world" ("Political World") that corrupts everyone and corrodes basic values. This sense that there now really is "no direction home" also pervades the despairing "Everything Is Broken." Nor does the pessimism lift in more recent work. In "Not Dark Yet," he offers a definite anti-Enlightenment take on his fellow humans, declaring that "my sense of humanity has gone down the drain," while in "Things Have Changed" we are told simply that "[p]eople are crazy and things are strange." If postmodernists are right that ideals are questionable, ambiguous, and self-defeating, then no overarching conception of progress is possible. Reason cannot guide us toward freedom.

Deconstructive Critique and Postmodern Paradoxes: Nothing to Win and Nothing to Lose?

A central misgiving about postmodern approaches is that they leave us without a standpoint from which to criticize existing society. Postmodernists contradict their conclusions in their actions, for they have been among the most vocal social critics. When postmodernists protest the use of Enlightenment ideals, they imply that we would be better off without these principles. Yet this entails that there are more and less valid political ideas. Postmodernists criticize the use of reason to pursue freedom, yet they also attempt to liberate us through reasoning. Defenders of the Enlightenment have argued that postmodernism is inherently contradictory, presupposing the ideals of reason and freedom which it criticizes.

Is there any way that postmodernism can allow for criticism and remain consistent? One approach is to simply describe social structures and the limits of reason while refraining from proposing reforms. Thus one avoids the paradox of asserting any vision of progress while denying the possibility of such. This is the image of the most bleak Dylan songs, "It's Alright, Ma (I'm Only Bleeding)," "Desolation Row," and "Ballad of a Thin Man," where no hope for escape from domination is offered. In "My Back Pages" Dylan's rejection of moral judgment remains consistent insofar as he makes no claim on other individuals or his society. He does not go on to say, as many relativists do, "Since there's no good and bad, we should all just tolerate each other." This would be self-contradictory, defending an action as right while denying the existence of right and wrong. By not drawing conclusions other than that none can be drawn, the contradiction is avoided. We might call this "descriptive postmodernism," as it makes no prescriptions for individuals or society.

Derrida and Foucault similarly attempt social criticism that makes no claim to fundamental moral or political truth. Derrida calls his approach deconstruction, as it reveals the ambiguity and power involved in claims to truth. Foucault refers to a similar critical stance as "problematization."[4] Rather than measuring society against an explicit ideal, he recommends showing that current ideals involve contradictions, ambiguities, and domination. Ultimately both thinkers hope that immanent criticism of problematic current ideals will open up new, unspecified social paths.

Yet, one might object that even problematization suggests some moral judgment. To suggest that current ideals should be rejected because of their ambivalent meaning and implications

---

[4] "Polemics, Politics, and Problematizations: An interview with Michel Foucault," in *The Foucault Reader*, pp. 381–390.

is to say that we should live free of false ideals and that we can pursue better alternatives. Even the assertion that all ideals are false and should not be followed suggests some understanding of the moral universe. Postmodernists have a lot to say for people who don't believe in truth.

The difficulty of avoiding commitment to Enlightenment ideals is apparent in Dylan. Despite his self-distancing from protest music, concerns for freedom and justice continue to underpin Dylan's work. Even the songs which portray society as exhaustively denying avenues of freedom—"It's Alright, Ma (I'm Only Bleeding)" and "Desolation Row"—are kinds of protest against poverty, materialism, and lack of individual freedom and opportunity. But this is to say that society is unjust and would be better were there more opportunities for securing individual well-being and self expression. Similarly, in "Political World" the lament that "[w]isdom is thrown in jail," "mercy walks the plank," and "courage is a thing of the past" coveys a commitment to these lost ideals, while the lament in "Dark Eyes" that "beauty goes unrecognized" certainly expresses a confidence that beauty does indeed exist.

While Dylan pens a few songs expressing extreme skepticism of political progress, his work continues to call for justice. Though *Another Side of Bob Dylan* introduces the relativism and political surrender of "My Back Pages," it also contains "Chimes of Freedom," which endorses a universal concern for human well-being and tolerance of difference. *Bringing It All Back Home* includes "Maggie's Farm," a song that proclaims a vision of freedom in its refusal to work under exploitative, senseless authoritarian conditions. Dylan's later work includes "Hurricane," a plea for justice in the case of Rubin "Hurricane" Carter, and "Señor," subtitled "Tales of Yankee Power," which analyzes corruption and community disintegration through the profit motive. "Union Sundown" has clear postmodern features as it expresses skepticism over the viability of a workers' movement that has become a "big business," but it also cries foul about unregulated capitalism which is "above the law" and the exploitation of third-world labor. Dylan's belief in universal moral truth is apparent in the 1990s when he searches everywhere for "Dignity." While Dylan has postmodern moments, these do not entirely dominate an album, much less his career.

Both Sides of Dylan and Politics

It's difficult to develop a coherent political stance around postmodern arguments. While social philosophers and critics, from Derrida to Dylan, express doubts about modern reason and institutions, they cannot consistently reject them. Postmodern insights are best appropriated as cautionary secondary principles guiding our interpretation and implementation of Enlightenment principles and institutions. Postmodern insights about tendencies for bias and ambiguity are useful reminders of the fallibility of reason and society. Yet, this does not mean that there are not better and worse principles and interpretations of these principles.

Dylan's work as a whole might be presented as an example of social criticism that combines cautious skepticism about modern ideals and institutions with protest that attempts to realize those ideals more fully and perfectly. Such self-criticism is part of the Enlightenment attempt to attain more genuine autonomy in our personal and political relationships. Continual deliberation and action aimed at progress are indispensable. Perhaps the thief in "All Along the Watchtower" says it best, emphasizing commitment in the face of confusion, skepticism, and ambivalence:

> There are many here among us who feel that life is but a joke
> But you and I, we've been through that, and this is not our
>   fate
> So let us not talk falsely now, the hour is getting late

7

"To Live Outside the Law, You Must Be Honest": Freedom in Dylan's Lyrics

ELIZABETH BRAKE

Bob Dylan stands for an ideal of personal freedom. He (or his lyrical persona) won't stick around in a bad situation ("Don't Think Twice, It's All Right"), consent to be owned ("It Ain't Me, Babe"), be someone's boss ("It Takes a Lot to Laugh, It Takes a Train to Cry"), try to please ("It's Alright, Ma (I'm Only Bleeding)"), answer reporters' clichéd questions, stick to folk songs, or work on Maggie's farm "no more." There are many things he won't do: but what will he do? This is a lot of negativity: if he just keeps on keeping on, where will he end up?

Starting with *Another Side of Bob Dylan*, Dylan turned from overtly political songs to songs of a personal nature. At a 1966 concert, someone shouted: "Play protest songs!" Dylan answered: "Oh come on, these are all protest songs. Aw, it's the same stuff as always. Can't you *hear*?" Then he played "Ballad of a Thin Man."[1] The "same stuff," apparently, was an assertion of freedom. These self-expressive, iconoclastic songs, written against folky expectations, tend to harp on rejecting the influence of others—lovers, families, "everybody [who] wants you to be just like them" ("Maggie's Farm," "To Ramona").

Sometimes, in these songs, there is an allegory of the personal to the political ("Maggie's Farm"). Sometimes, Dylan takes a critical view of political protest, that it remains empty so long as it remains abstract ("My Back Pages"), and that the political

---

[1] Mike Marqusee, *Chimes of Freedom: The Politics of Bob Dylan's Art* (New York: The New Press, 2003), p. 199.

rhetoric of freedom can itself impede freedom. The songs insist on lawlessness and change, unleashing the chaotic and carnivalesque both lyrically and musically. But what kind of freedom is Dylan talking about?

"To live outside the law, you must be honest." Why? Outside *what* law? Is there another law, mandating honesty, outside the law? In this chapter, I will look at the notion of freedom as Dylan develops it in four albums of this period—*Another Side of Bob Dylan, Bringing It All Back Home, Highway 61 Revisited,* and *Blonde on Blonde*—bringing us finally to this extra-legal imperative of honesty.[2]

Negation

Over and over, Dylan casts himself as outlaw, as the negation of whatever society expects or requires, as judge and satirist of the *status quo*. Distanced from society, he questions its values and refuses, at least imaginatively, to conform to its standards. He does this by moving on, taking to the road and leaving lovers and rules behind. The outlaw rejects possessive love, a fixed abode, regular work, social niceties, and authority of law.

This persona often defines himself through negatives—as what he is *not*, does *not* want, does *not* have—as opposed to what he *is, wants,* and *has*. The only thing we know for sure about this figure is that he has his freedom. But my question is what this freedom is, if not merely a series of negations, as in "It Ain't Me, Babe": "But it ain't me, babe / No, no, no, it ain't me, babe." Here the singer defines himself by what he rejects, what he is *not* (compare "I'll Keep It With Mine": "I'm not loving you for what you are / But for what you're not"). His lyrics spurn political and religious authority, norms of behavior, work, schooling, gift-giving, social scenes, love—targeting most of what might be taken to give structure and meaning to life.

In the songs from this period, resistance is enacted through self-exile, removal, and refusal: "you ask why I don't live here / Honey, how come you don't move?" ("On the Road Again"). The singer hands in his notice at Maggie's Farm and refuses to accept

---

[2] In later work, which I don't consider here, Dylan continues to explore the nature and conditions of freedom.

any letters not from Desolation Row. Even "Mona Lisa musta had the highway blues" ("Visions of Johanna"). There's no plan—"Where I'm bound, I can't tell" ("Don't Think Twice, It's All Right")—except not to stay, not to conform. (What happens to conformists? "You follow, find yourself at war" ["It's Alright, Ma (I'm Only Bleeding)"]).

If we look for constructive proposals as to how to live, we find striking insistence on change:

> Well, I wish I was on some
> Australian mountain range
> I got no reason to be there, but I
> Imagine it would be some kind of change ("Outlaw Blues")

Moving on is the imperative of liberation: "You must leave now" and "go start anew": "Leave your stepping stones behind, something calls for you / Forget the dead you've left, they will not follow you"("It's All Over Now, Baby Blue"). Following this, there appears a "vagabond who's rapping at your door," dressed "in the clothes that you once wore"—the implication being that the vagabond is the next stage in your development. One must leave everything and then change oneself.

This is why "Like a Rolling Stone" is not simply vindictive, but, as Mike Marqusee writes, a ballad of "potential liberation."[3] It depicts the disorientation that occurs when, without wealth and friends, the individual is forced onto her own resources:

> on your own
> With no direction home
> Like a complete unknown
> Like a rolling stone

Exile releases: "When you got nothing, you got nothing to lose." Previously the addressee "never understood that it ain't no good" to use others and live vicariously, but now, exiled from the "pretty people / . . . drinkin', thinkin' that they got it made," she sees the falseness of that position. However, freedom can't be *merely* exile. Not all outcasts are free: many inhabitants of

---

[3] Marqusee, p. 156.

Desolation Row and the down-trodden in "Chimes of Freedom" are in the grip of tyranny. What then does freedom consist in?

The outlaw blues offer no positive advice, no constructive ideal. Injunctions not to conform can't, by their nature, tell us what to be. These proposals for freedom focus on avoiding external social constraints, not on becoming someone specific (for example, a yogi). To some philosophers, this emphasis is just. The history of philosophy contains a debate over two competing understandings of freedom, negative freedom and positive freedom, a contrast famously illuminated by Isaiah Berlin in his 1958 essay, "Two Concepts of Liberty."[4] Berlin argued that political liberty should be understood as negative freedom, or non-interference: "Political liberty in this sense is simply the area within which a man can act unobstructed by others."[5] Thus, I am free when I don't face external impediments, imposed by others, to doing what I wish.

Negative freedom, or liberty as non-interference, is a classical liberal ideal in politics, defended by John Stuart Mill in *On Liberty* (1869). The state should not interfere with one's liberty to act, so long as one doesn't intrude on others. But as a personal ideal, this looks inadequate. A drug addict may be politically free, insofar as he is not imprisoned, but fail to be fully free due to his addiction. When his desire for drugs drives him, despite his strong wishes to clean up, to his dealer, this inner compulsion seems to deprive him of freedom. Likewise, although Dylan's "outlaw blues" suggest an ideal of negative freedom, this isn't the whole story: for Dylan, understanding freedom as "freedom to do whatever one wants, without external interference" is unsatisfactory. Desires can be conformist. Dylan doesn't seem to think that freedom is achieved when the individual is able to do as she wishes—his songs catalogue petty wants and parasitic desires.

When we consider that people may have compulsive or inauthentic desires, negative freedom seems inadequate. Its competing ideal of positive freedom may then seem more attractive. Positive freedom, as Berlin explains it, is the ability to con-

---

[4] Isaiah Berlin, "Two Concepts of Liberty," in his *Four Essays on Liberty* (Oxford: Oxford University Press, 1970), pp. 118–172.
[5] Berlin, p. 122.

trol oneself, mastering one's worse—irrational, addicted—self. Often, theories of positive freedom hold that individuals possess higher and lower selves, and that state interference is required to help individuals subdue their lower selves, leading to state authoritarianism. Thus, Berlin criticized self-realization as a *political* ideal, arguing that the state should not *compel* us to realize ourselves—it should merely leave us alone.

The most attractive view, then, may be that we should have negative freedom politically, guaranteeing our freedom of action, and an ideal of self-realization, which shares with positive freedom the emphasis on becoming something specific, at the personal level. Mill propounded such a theory of human nature, arguing that negative liberty in the political realm was necessary for our self-realization, the expression of our authentic selves. (In contrast, theorists of positive liberty often contend that this combination is impossible, and that the essential self is social.)[6] According to Mill, negative liberty—including free speech and free action, freedom of assembly and conscience— is the condition for self-realization.

The *personal* ideal of freedom as self-realization chimes with Dylan's broadsides against the "pretty people": after all, freedom of action (negative freedom) is compatible with enslavement to conformity. If the "pretty people" lack freedom, they must lack it in the sense of self-realization. Conversely, someone imprisoned may be free, in the sense of self-realization, in his mind ("I Shall Be Released"). Freedom for Dylan, then, is not the same thing as freedom from interference; however, given his critique of convention, we may think that, like Mill, he takes negative liberty to be a condition for attaining freedom in the sense of self-realization.

This is a good thing, since the failings of Dylan's outlaw creed (which sounds like a statement of negative freedom) become clear when viewed through the lens of a famous critic of negative freedom, nineteenth century philosopher Georg Hegel. As developed by Hegel, the contrast between negative

---

[6] For more on this and other issues related to positive and negative liberty, see Carter, Ian, "Positive and Negative Liberty," in Edward N. Zalta, ed., *The Stanford Encyclopedia of Philosophy* (Spring 2003 Edition), http://plato .stanford.edu/archives/spr2003/entries/liberty-positive-negative/ (accessed January 18th, 2005).

and positive freedom was between, on the one hand, refusing social norms, and on the other, internalizing them. Hegel excoriated what he called "negative freedom" or "the freedom of the void." As he defined it, this involves the human ability to distance ourselves from our particular characteristics. For any characteristic (such as height or nationality), I can imagine myself without it. Hegel calls this "the I's" pure reflection into itself, in which every limitation, every content . . . is dissolved."[7] Since the thinking self seems to exist independently of all characteristics (except being a thinking self), it is not defined by them. Hegel writes that, psychologically, "I am able to free myself from everything, to renounce all ends, and to abstract from everything. The human being alone is able to abandon all things, even his own life."[8]

From the perspective of the indeterminate "I," any label or definition seems limiting. Consequently, freedom is understood as rejecting such limitations, especially social conventions. This is what Hegel calls negative freedom. It is premised on rejection. Dylan's negative formulations posit just such a freedom: "it is not he or she or them or it / That you belong to" ("It's Alright, Ma (I'm Only Bleeding)"). But to Hegel, this is an inadequate understanding of freedom. If one had no limitations, belonged to nothing, there would be no one to be free. To be a person at all, one must define oneself. Otherwise, one is purely reactive. Negative freedom risks nothingness or destructiveness: "Only in destroying something does this negative will have a feeling of its own existence." Negativity, in other words, can't pull you through ("Just Like Tom Thumb's Blues").

For Hegel, this is because the self is inherently social; one couldn't exist in a vacuum, without language or customs. Consider an outlaw. The role of outlaw is socially defined; it exists as opposition to law-abiding society, and its meaning is given by resonance in song and myth. While Dylan's outlaw persona flirts with negative freedom, it is still a socially defined role.

Dylan seems to recognize that negative freedom, in Hegel's sense, is unattainable: "'Are birds free from the chains of the

---

[7] G.W.F. Hegel, *Elements of the Philosophy of Right* (Cambridge: Cambridge University Press, 1995 [1821]), p. 37, par. 5.
[8] Hegel, p. 38, par. 5.

skyway?'" ("Ballad in Plain D"). Experience tethers us as the sky tethers the birds, setting parameters on flight. Yet he also seems to think that some measure of negation is an important condition of freedom.

Affirmation

Dylan's work suggests an imperative of self-realization: "he not busy being born is busy dying" ("It's Alright, Ma (I'm Only Bleeding)").[9] Exile, it seems, allows the birth of an authentic (as opposed to social, artificial) self. The concept of an authentic self is difficult: is it innate, waiting to be released, or must it be created? If the latter, what gives it authenticity? For now, these questions can be set aside. Dylan offers an epistemology of the self, an account of how we come to know it, rather than a metaphysics, or an account of what the self is.

While Hegel sees the self as dependent on society, Dylan sees it as radically independent of, and constrained by, society. This stands in the tradition of American Transcendentalist Ralph Waldo Emerson, as well as the Romantic notion of spontaneity reflected in Mill's *On Liberty*. Emerson's essay, "Self-Reliance," provides a classic articulation of this view.[10]

Emerson suggests that society threatens selfhood: "the voices which we hear in solitude . . . grow faint and inaudible as we enter into the world. Society everywhere is in conspiracy against the manhood of every one of its members" (p. 133). Only through defying convention can we achieve independence: "Whoso would be a man must be a nonconformist" (p. 133) because only the habit of independence can preserve the inner voice. Even success endangers individuality: a man "is weaker by every recruit to his banner" (p. 150). Likewise, Dylan suggests that the self appears in solitude:

---

[9] Later, Dylan's allusions to rebirth will invoke a different kind of being "born again." Perhaps this traces a continuing preoccupation between the younger, more skeptical Dylan and the fundamentalist Christian.

[10] Ralph Waldo Emerson, "Self-Reliance," in *Ralph Waldo Emerson*, edited by Richard Poirier (Oxford: Oxford University Press, 1990), pp. 131–151. Hereafter cited parenthetically in text.

You lose yourself, you reappear
You suddenly find you got nothing to fear
Alone you stand with nobody near ("It's Alright, Ma (I'm
  Only Bleeding)")

Emerson doesn't call for isolation ("the great man is he who in
the midst of the crowd keeps with perfect sweetness the independence of solitude" [p. 150]) but for independence in judgment. Such judgment attaches to persons and beliefs and
involves evaluation. Although timidity leads persons to dismiss
their insights—the "Emperor's new clothes" phenomenon—
Emerson claims that "the healthy attitude of human nature" is the

> nonchalance of boys who are sure of a dinner . . .A boy is in the
> parlour what the pit is in the playhouse; independent, irresponsi-
> ble, looking out from his corner on such people and facts as pass
> by, he tries and sentences them on their merits, in the swift, sum-
> mary way of boys. (p. 133)

A similar insistence of independence is found in Dylan.
Though everybody wants him "to be just like them," he insists
that he "be just like I am" ("Maggie's Farm"). Self-realization
involves evaluating people and situations independently, resist-
ing evaluations others would impose. Every law and judgment
(juridical, moral, social) must be open to questioning, placing
one, in a sense, outside the law: as Emerson wrote, "No law can
be sacred to me but that of my nature. Good and bad are but
names . . . the only right is what is after my constitution" (p.
134).
    Dylan too rejects simplifying categories. "Lies that life is black
and white" ("My Back Pages") replace experience with second-
hand desire:

The kingdoms of Experience
In the precious wind they rot
While paupers change possessions
Each one wishing for what the other has got ("Gates of
  Eden")

Thus he declares his good intentions in "All I Really Want to
Do": not to "[s]implify you, classify you," or to "[a]nalyze you,

categorize you." One must receive experience unmediated by others' classifications: "Take what you have gathered from coincidence" ("It's All Over Now, Baby Blue"). Independent judgment will be complex, unsimplified.

Let's look again at the catalogue of conformities which Dylan rejects. These "false gods" ("It's Alright, Ma (I'm Only Bleeding)") usurp individual judgment. They simplify, manipulate desire, project value where it's not and hide it where it is, play carrot-and-stick with the donkey of autonomy, and they are exploited by kings, ads, friends, lovers. It's no organized conspiracy that Dylan depicts, but a society requiring such deforming conformities (work, love, manners) that its successes are deprived of their wit (Mr. Jones) and seek a sense of self in superiority (the parasites). First, possessive love:

> Relationships of ownership
> They whisper in the wings
> To those condemned to act accordingly
> And wait for succeeding kings ("Gates of Eden")

Victims have an urge to be owned, to wait for kings, to abdicate self-sovereignty. Even in "Desolation Row," possessive love will not be tolerated:

> And in comes Romeo, he's moaning
> "You Belong To Me I Believe"
> And someone says, "You're in the wrong place, my friend
> You better leave"

Social approval and acceptance carry absurd costs:

> It's all just a dream, babe
> A vacuum, a scheme, babe
> That sucks you into feelin' like this ("To Ramona")

Ramona's enemies are the "forces and friends" who "type" her, "Making you feel / That you must be exactly like them." She sees *herself* through their projections. Not surprising, since some themselves "[b]ent out of shape from society's pliers" ("It's Alright, Ma (I'm Only Bleeding)") manipulate others to gain a sense of superiority: in "Ballad in Plain D," a jealous "parasite" tyrannizes her "scapegoat" sister: "Countless visions of the other she'd reflect / As a crutch for her scenes and her society." Parasites feed on others for self-esteem; they lack a sense of self. Parasites, users, and crutches keep reappearing ("Visions of Johanna," "Subterranean Homesick Blues," "Fourth Time Around," "From a Buick 6").

Duty and success form another set of illusions. Government and greedy capitalists exploit and oppress ("Bob Dylan's 115th Dream," "Subterranean Homesick Blues," "Maggie's Farm," "Highway 61 Revisited," "Tombstone Blues," "It's Alright, Ma (I'm Only Bleeding)"), but they are enabled to do so by illusions which sustain obedience: Maggie's Ma "talks to all the servants / About man and God and law." People seek "to be a success / Please her, please him, buy gifts," but hard work doesn't pay: "Twenty years of schoolin' / And they put you on the day shift" ("Subterranean Homesick Blues"). The wise woman of "Love Minus Zero," in contrast, "knows there's no success like failure / And that failure's no success at all."

Dylan's barbs aren't only for the greedy and cruel, but also the pretentious, the naïve, anyone who abdicates their judgment in favor of prefabricated categories: "You've been with the professors / and they've all liked your looks" ("Ballad of a Thin Man"). Pieties—academic or political—are mocked:

> Now, I'm liberal, but to a degree
> I want ev'rybody to be free
> But if you think that I'll let Barry Goldwater
> Move in next door and marry my daughter
> You must think I'm crazy! ("I Shall Be Free No. 10")

Or,

> A self-ordained professor's tongue
> Too serious to fool
> Spouted out that liberty
> Is just equality in school ("My Back Pages")

In Dylan's meta-political critique, abstract labels—"liberal"—permit hypocrisy and superficiality. What binds the worshippers of these false gods is a failure to think for themselves. Some are deceived, others apathetically "obey authority" without respecting it ("It's Alright, Ma (I'm Only Bleeding)"). Their "sin," like Ophelia's, is a certain kind of "lifelessness" ("Desolation Row").

How does this relate to freedom? Dylan draws a society which will control you by getting you to conform. Forces opposed to your independence—government, business, friends, lovers—undermine it psychologically. Against this, Dylan— barely—suggests an idea of self-realization, the necessary con- dition for which is detaching from society. Being yourself is easier said than done: we can see how Dylan is defined by his reaction against these forces, the things he rebels against them- selves determine his response, making his contempt a crutch.

Synthesis

Self-realization requires going outside society's law. Yet there is still another law. My title comes from "Absolutely Sweet Marie":

> But to live outside the law, you must be honest
> I know you always say that you agree
> But where are you tonight, sweet Marie?

The dig at Marie strikes at hypocrisy, but also suggests a con- cluding thought.

Notice that the honesty required outside the law is intersub- jective: Marie has failed to be honest to Dylan (not to herself). We should expect free relationships outside the law to consist in undistorted acceptance of the other ("I never tried to change you in any way" ["She's Your Lover Now"]). But Dylan's songs in this period reflect betrayal. Outside the law, without positions and possessions to prop the ego, persons are vulnerable, and relationships can be destructive as well as liberating. When out- laws deceive or exploit each other, there's no social structure, no comforting illusion (such as blame) in the background (per- haps this is why the song ends "in the ruins" of Marie's balcony). The gain from leaving the precincts of the law is the possibility of achieving a certain independence of thought; the risk is vul- nerability.

Self-realization brings a second, self-regarding law: that of one's own nature. The demands of freedom are severe. Its achievement involves more than merely rejecting social norms. Many philosophers have questioned the value of social status, material goods, and conventional morality. But Emerson—and Dylan (and others: Friedrich Nietzsche and the existentialists)— are insistent in holding that the law which replaces these is not objectively specifiable, and, indeed, that it is more rigorous than conventional morality.

The "law of consciousness," in Emerson's phrase, is hard: "If any one imagines that this law is lax, let him keep its commandment one day" (p. 144). The difficulty lies in recognizing and trusting one's independent judgment. If one is a law unto oneself, no other law provides guidance, support, justification. Thus Emerson commands, "Trust thyself"—echoed in Dylan's 1985 song, "Trust yourself," and his advice "To Ramona": "Do what you think you must do."

It's not just self-trust that's difficult. Society's illusions also comfort. Thus Nietzsche, disappointed by Lou Andreas von Salomé, wrote: "She told me herself that she had no morality— and I thought she had, like myself, a more severe morality than anybody."[11] We can imagine why Nietzsche, juxtaposing conventional morality with a self-determined code of behavior, should think the former, with its potential for hypocrisy, displacement of responsibility, and self-aggrandizement, less demanding. Honesty to oneself, it appears, may be a more exacting law than those the outlaw leaves behind.[12]

---

[11] In a draft letter to Paul Rée, 1882. Friedrich Nietzsche, *Sämtliche Briefe* (Berlin: de Gruyter), p. 309.
[12] I wish to thank Mark Migotti, Zayne Reeves, and Peter Vernezze for very helpful comments on earlier drafts of this chapter.

8

We Call It a Snake: Dylan Reclaims the Creative Word

RUVIK DANIELI and ANAT BILETZKI

"Man Gave Names to All the Animals" is the penultimate song on Bob Dylan's 1979 album *Slow Train Coming*, which is generally considered to have heralded the Jewish-born songwriter's embrace of Jesus Christ and Christianity. Each verse consists of three lines describing an animal and a fourth, payoff line giving the animal's name, followed by a simple, catchy chorus. It is perhaps no wonder, then, that some have mistaken this deceptive song for a child's ditty, a rock-era variation on "Old MacDonald Had a Farm." But to ascribe merely a juvenile intent to "Man Gave Names to All the Animals" is to miss this metaphysical poet at his most profound, just as he comes to question the very possibility of conveying his meaning—or any, for that matter.

Even without taking into account the personal circumstances surrounding the making of the album, Dylan's so-called conversion to Christianity, his inspiration for the song clearly seems to have come from the Bible; to be more specific, from the Old Testament creation story. The chorus almost literally echoes the verses in Genesis (2:19–20):

> And out of the ground the Lord God formed every beast of the field, and every fowl of the air; and brought them unto the man to see what he would call them: and whatsoever the man called every living creature, that was the name thereof. And *the man gave names* to all cattle, and to the fowl of the air, and to every beast of the field.

Through this biblical citation alone Dylan could be understood to be speaking about some rather hefty metaphysical issues: man's essential nature as the *namer* of things, the relationship between man and the brute (or mute) creation, and that between man and God—all of which appear to subsist in or through language, the poet's tool.

But let's not get ahead of ourselves. The chorus may perhaps demarcate the field of Dylan's interest, but not the point he's trying to make. For that we have to return to the song's seemingly innocuous verses. In the manner of a children's song, they repetitively build up a picture of the procedure the biblical verses describe, as each in turn presents a different animal by its attributes and man names it ("bear," "bull," "sheep," "cow," "pig"). There is an anomaly, however: the last verse is missing the payoff line; the song breaks off abruptly, and man never gets around to naming that animal which is "smooth as glass" and "slither[s] . . . through the grass," only to "disappear in a tree near a lake." The failure to name what could only be the snake isn't just an accidental or idiosyncratic way to end the song. It's the real payoff: the point to which the entire song is leading.

No Naming an Animal as Smooth as Glass

What does it mean to give a name? In the narrow biblical context, within the Jewish and Christian exegetical tradition, giving a name always and invariably signifies the dominion of the name-giver over the thing or person named. To give a name implies lordship.[1] It's an idea Dylan may have encountered as

---

[1] This general principle is explicitly stated already in the creation story, with God telling man (Genesis 1:28) that he is to "have dominion over" the animals to which he will presently be giving names, and over woman whom he in fact names twice (Genesis 2:23, 3:20). Throughout the Bible, we find that man's name-giving function is exercised most frequently by parents naming their offspring and in the giving of place-names as constituting ownership. This notion was shared by other nations as well: Egypt's Pharaoh renamed Joseph (Genesis 41:39–45); Pharaoh Necho of Egypt and Nebuchadnezzar king of Babylon renamed their puppets on the throne of the kingdom of Judah (2 Kings 23:34, 24:17); the Chaldean "prince of the eunuchs" renamed the prophet Daniel and his three Jewish companions (Daniel 1:3–7); and, in the New Testament Jesus renamed Simon Peter, his designated successor and

early as Jewish Sunday school classes in his childhood in
Hibbing. Or he may have become familiar with it at this junc-
ture of his life, with religion, as a matter of record, having come
to the fore. Likely it is an idea that intrigued him, being somebody who in a sense became master of his own destiny by
renaming himself. In all probability, he would not have
employed it lightly, for some mere trifling purpose.

What of the snake, then, this animal that Dylan will not
name? Again in a narrow biblical context, within the Jewish and
Christian tradition, the snake represents one thing only: he is the
serpent in the Garden of Eden, the source of original sin, the
author of man's fall from divine grace and expulsion from paradise. From him stems everything that is evil in man. This snake
of the creation story was "the primeval serpent," from whom the
evil inclination draws its strength. In Jewish religious doctrine,
the evil inclination is an innate component in man, which he
must master and overcome. This is the snake, and Dylan won't
name it.

So, taken in a narrow biblical context, purely within the religious tradition, Dylan's song seems to be sending a simple but
trenchant message: man does *not* have dominion over his evil
inclination. With the song breaking off abruptly just as it makes
this point, the ensuing silence seems to imply that the exact
opposite holds true, and it is the evil inclination that has dominion over man. This is a depressing conclusion and a melancholy
message, but a legitimate interpretation nevertheless. How can
we refrain from accepting it as what Dylan may have been trying to say?

We can, first, take into account both the whole of the album
in which the song is embedded and the acknowledged circumstances of its writing and making. These might conveniently be

---

some of his disciples (Matthew 16:18, Mark 3:14–19, Luke 6:13–16).
Furthermore, the principle of establishing lordship through name-giving is
most evident when God himself names or renames chosen individuals, such
as Israel's three patriarchs—Abraham, Isaac, and Jacob (Genesis 17:5, 19;
35:10). The prophets Isaiah and Hosea were told which names to give their
children by God (Isaiah 8:1–3; Hosea 1:4–9). Finally, Joseph the carpenter and
his wife Mary and Zacharias the priest were instructed by an angel of God to
name their respective sons John and Jesus (Matthew 1:21, Luke 1:13, 31). Most
explicit and succinct is a single biblical verse: "But now saith the Lord that created thee . . . I have called thee by thy name, thou art mine" (Isaiah 43:1).

summarized as Dylan's so-called conversion to Christianity, a religion that holds out the optimistic hope of ultimate salvation and redemption through the figure of Jesus Christ. In one of the album's other songs, "When You Gonna Wake Up?" Dylan clearly indicates that he, at least, is well aware of this symbolic function and significance of the Christ figure. And indeed, in what seems to be a contrapuntal juxtaposition, the next song after "Man Gave Names to All the Animals," the concluding song of the album, is "When He Returns," which might be construed as referring to this hope and this figure of salvation, perhaps in a deliberate attempt to ameliorate the harshly despondent message of its predecessor.

If standing on its own, then, the song's message is nothing beyond the stark and uncompromising assertion of man's subjection to his own evil inclination, this simply doesn't jibe with, and in fact actually belies, the tenor of the entire album. From the very first song—even from the name of the album—there is a sense that the choice between good and evil is man's to make, and there are grave consequences to the choice he makes (explicitly spoken of in "Gotta Serve Somebody," "Gonna Change My Way Of Thinking," "Do Right To Me Baby (Do Unto Others)," and "When You Gonna Wake Up?"). So the proposed interpretation of "Man Gave Names to All the Animals" appears to accord neither with Dylan's ostensibly optimistic adoption of Jesus Christ and Christianity into his basically Jewish worldview, nor with the positive attitude consistent with such optimism that is expressed by the album's other songs. Let's leave biblical exegesis and go on, then, to the philosophy of language.

In the Beginning

Let's recall that biblical citation with which we began this inquiry. Did we not say that on its own it raises the hefty metaphysical question concerning man's essential nature as a *namer* of things, and that in the larger context of the procedure described it also deals with the relationships between man and the brute (or mute) creation and between man and God, which subsist in or through language? Is it conceivable that Dylan, being a poet highly sensitive to the repercussions of his words, having taken his inspiration directly from this passage in Genesis, and having so faithfully reproduced the experience of the biblical procedure described in it in the progression of his song towards its sad conclusion, could really have been unaware of these issues? Are they to be so lightly dismissed in attempting to ascertain his meaning in "Man Gave Names to All the Animals"? We think not.

In order to go about examining these issues, we introduce another thinker and another text into this discussion. The thinker is Walter Benjamin, and the text is "On Language as Such and on the Language of Man," written in 1916 and unpublished in Benjamin's lifetime.[2] Like Dylan, Benjamin takes his inspiration from the Bible, constructing his analysis of language around the creation story in general and man's naming of the animals in particular.

Benjamin asserts that language is all communication of the contents of the mind; man communicates his own mental being by *naming* all other things: *language as such is the mental being of man.* There is an immediate and unmediated relation between name and thing named, because human language has a "magical community with things [that] is immaterial and purely mental, and the symbol of this is sound" (p. 67). Thus Benjamin is in agreement with the Bible "in presupposing language as an ultimate reality, perceptible only in its manifestation, inexplicable and mystical" (p. 67). Here, we feel, is a definition that would resonate handsomely with Dylan.

Against this background, Benjamin begins to examine the biblical creation story, sketching a three-tier hierarchical order consisting of God, man, and the mute creation—all three linked through language. Creation begins with the creative omnipotence of language and ends with language's assimilation of the created by naming it. By the word of God was the creation made; man, however, who was not created from the word, has been invested by God with the gift of language and thus elevated above nature, above the brute and mute creation. It is man's task, expressly assigned to him by God, to name things: by his naming, man becomes God's partner in creation and completes the conjuration of the world into being.

---

[2] In *Walter Benjamin: Selected Writings Volume I, 1913–1926* (Cambridge, Massachusetts: Harvard University Press), pp. 62–74. Hereafter cited parenthetically in text.

Long Time Ago

But note: we are dealing with a song that bespeaks a failure of language, a lapse in its creativity, a breakdown in its ability to name things and conjure them into being. This breakdown takes place in a very specific context: the naming of the snake, the source of man's evil inclination, who enticed the woman to eat from the fruit of "the tree of the knowledge of good and evil" (Genesis 2:17), thus bringing about man's and woman's expulsion from the Garden of Eden, their fall from divine grace, and their passage out of an original paradisiacal state. Just as Dylan comes to mention this tree, the snake disappears in it before man can name the beast. If the snake, then, has not been conjured into being through his naming in man's name-language, how could he possibly entice the woman to eat from the fruit of the tree of knowledge? To judge by the song, the tree might be standing there innocently in its lakeside prospect, its pendulous fruits still hanging untouched from its branches outspread over the water, and the only suggestion of a possible Fall a small twinge of apprehension at the sight of an indistinct serpentine shadow slithering through its leaves. Could Dylan be trying to intimate that this was no failure of language but rather its success in avoiding the Fall? Or is he saying, perhaps, that it was no success at all?

Benjamin, somewhat contradictorily, identifies an *immediate* lapse in the creativity of man's name-language; he says that it has lost the divine actuality of God's creative word, the creative power of which has turned to knowledge: "Man is the knower in the same language as God is the creator" (p. 68), albeit "the naming word in the knowledge of man . . . must fall short of the creative word of God" (p. 70). And yet, he tells us also that revelation is the only mental region in which man "does not know the inexpressible" (p. 67), which is almost by definition exactly where language ceases to function. Benjamin, then, nevertheless appears to sustain the notion of an absolute accord between God's creative word and man's name-language in the primeval, paradisiacal past, when there was complete correspondence between the contents of man's mind and the divine creation—of which man's naming the animals is the most potent symbol. It is an accord that can now be recovered only through revelation, which sidesteps any need of prior knowledge.

So Benjamin traces a progression, or regression, from that point at which man was the knower in the same language as God was the creator to what he now designates as the "human word." When and how did this "human word" become separate and distinct from man's original name-language, which, as the vehicle of "perfect knowledge," was identical with the creative word of God? Here Benjamin, like Dylan, ultimately arrives at the tree of knowledge of good and evil.

I Think I Won't Call It a Snake

In passing from "perfect knowledge" to "the knowledge of good and evil" that is the Fall, Benjamin performs a simplistic ploy similar to Dylan's, meanwhile taking a leap of faith out of linguistic theory into the realm of ethics and morality. Having already acknowledged that God is no less a knower through and in language than he is a creator through and in language, Benjamin asserts that since God has seen, cognized, knows, and named his creation to be "good" (Genesis 1:31), only "good" can have any real existence; since "evil" was never named, by either God or man, it doesn't exist in "perfect knowledge," which is man's, and God's, original state!

Finally, the snake is ready to make his appearance in Benjamin's essay, if not yet in Dylan's song:

> The knowledge to which the snake seduces, that of good and evil, is nameless . . . [and] is itself the only evil known to the paradisiacal state. Knowledge of good and evil abandons name; it is a knowledge from outside, the uncreated imitation of the creative word. (p. 71)

Having taken his leap of faith, Benjamin now introduces a new concept that could not have come into existence if both "good" and "evil" had not been named and conjured into being beforehand. This is the concept of "judgment," and it is man being judged. As name is a level of language equivalent to perfect knowledge, judgment, then, is an aspect or level of language equivalent to the knowledge of good and evil. Choice is implied, contrary to the immutable community of thing and word in man's primeval name-language.

This issue of choice is almost summarily concluded by Benjamin in his final paragraph on the Fall:

Good and bad, being unnameable and nameless, stand outside the language of names, which man leaves behind precisely in the abyss opened by this question . . . The Tree of Knowledge stood in the garden of God not in order to dispense information on good and evil, but as *an emblem of judgment over the questioner.* (p. 72, italics added)

Here then, it seems, we are finally told when perfect knowledge turns to the knowledge of good and evil, when man's name-language is corrupted into the human word and is divested of its communion with the creative word of God: it is when man ceases to *name* and begins to *question.*

Man Gave a Name to a Lake

In "Man Gave Names to All the Animals," man is still the namer; we must conclude that for Dylan he still is endowed with perfect knowledge, and in its total correspondence with God's creative word, man's name-language is its metaphysical complement and absolutely necessary for the completion of creation. Where man ceases to be the namer, says Benjamin, is exactly that moment when the snake puts forward its temptation and man takes it; in the song, however, man cannot name the snake—he does not take the lure, does not abandon perfect knowledge for the knowledge of good and evil. He may have ceased naming, but only in order to avoid becoming a questioner, to potentially become a namer again, to reunite the name he gives with the creative word of God in the divine actuality of creation. To Dylan, like any true poet, this is exactly his self-imposed (and perhaps divinely ordained) task: in revelation, not to *know* the inexpressible—in the second sense of knowing, the knowledge of good and evil, where to know is to question—but to recreate the inviolability of the word, the divine word; though merely a man, to speak words that recapture the divine actuality of those spoken by prophets in biblical times (recall that it is one of them, namely Jesus, with whom Dylan was much preoccupied at this time) and reestablish the absolute relation of name to knowledge.

So, although the point to which "Man Gave Names to All the Animals" is leading seems to bespeak a failure of language, a lapse in its creativity, a breakdown in its ability to name things and conjure them into being—to the contrary, the title of the song, its repetitive chorus, and the procedure it re-enacts all reaffirm language's creative potency and declare the possibility of its realization. These things celebrate the divine actuality which the human word aspires to, must aspire to, when it is uttered by prophets in the name of God or by poets and singer-songwriters in the name of revelation. Benjamin contends that this was what the human word of its own right aspired to before the degradation of perfect knowledge to the knowledge of good and evil, to questioning knowledge and judgment, when God had seen that his creation was good and called it such, and so evil could not have existed. Nevertheless, the point to which the song leads does indeed bespeak a failure or breakdown of language, which takes place in a very specific context: the naming of the snake. So whether we approach Dylan's song through the religious tradition or in the light of Benjamin's essay, one thing he clearly seems to be saying is that man needs to resist the snake's enticement and avoid the knowledge of good and evil. In the Jewish and Christian religious tradition, this could naively mean to subdue the evil inclination before it has even had a chance to be aroused. In the light of Benjamin's essay, it could mean, more intricately, to prevent knowledge from turning into judgment, to keep name from becoming debased into the judging word, to recapture man's requisite metaphysical stature as a namer and not become mired in uncreated imitation of the creative word as a questioner.

Seen in this light, then, in "Man Gave Names to All the Animals" Dylan yet again performs a conjurer's trick: he doesn't name the snake, the aboriginal questioner, but by placing his ultimate emphasis on *not* naming the questioner he implies that the questioner is there, that he might even be Dylan himself. Even as Dylan gives expression to every poet's desire to recapture that divine, creative immediacy of language and thus forge a new, perhaps better, reality, he is at the same time bemoaning every poet's—certainly every prophet's—inevitable destiny: to ultimately fail simply for having tried.

Finally, Dylan leaves us with the image of a lake. Those who still believe this is merely a child's ditty might maintain that the only reason we are left with this image is because it rhymes with snake; but those who take this poet more seriously might again look upon it as the deliberate selection of a word. It is an image that summons many attributes to mind: a surface beneath which lurk arcane depths and mysteries; a basic reflectivity, yet subject to moody changes according to season and circumstance; and in the circumstances of the song, a lake that sustains life around its shores.

Think of this one word; this one logos; this single linguistic creative act. Think of language as an ultimate reality, perceptible only in its manifestation, inexplicable and mystical. Recall that human language has a magical community with things that is immaterial and purely mental, and its symbol is sound. This lake, this sound Dylan leaves us with, resonates with the purity of language, a purity not yet violated by the sundering apart of word and name. Not being followed by any other sound, by any further linguistic creativity, it can be followed only by an absence of language—perhaps the true sin to which the song itself alludes. But in that absence, that silence, the sound yet continues to resound; there is no denying what is real.

Ultimately, in his song Dylan is trying to regain the lost creative omnipotence of the human word; to reclaim the *logos*. In not naming the snake, in suspending the Fall, Dylan is trying to bring us back to perfect knowledge, telling us to abandon the judgmental knowledge of good and evil, the uncreated imitation of the creative word.[3]

---

[3] The authors would like to acknowledge and express their gratitude to Helen Choi for the indispensable Benjamin connection.

Side 2

9

Bob Dylan's Truth

MICHAEL CHIARIELLO

In a famous scene from *Don't Look Back* (1966) Bob Dylan is being interviewed by a writer for *Time* magazine.[1] We see a cheeky Dylan upbraiding the hapless writer and his magazine for not being interested in printing "the real truth." "What is the real truth?" the writer challenges. Dylan responds, "The truth is just a plain picture of a tramp vomiting, man, into the sewer . . ."

The response might seem a theatrical gesture of youthful revolt against a major Establishment media prop. But when Dylan deployed surreal but concrete poetic imagery to undermine the "reasonable" journalist's sense of reality, there was more than theatre here. There was philosophy.[2] This last point is suggested by the journalist's retort, a rhetorical question: "Do you care about what you are saying?" Dylan loses his cool and retreats with the last word: "Each of us really knows nothing, but we all think we know things. But we know nothing." But I think Dylan was serious, and in a most novel way issues a critique of

---

[1] The reporter's name, Horace Judson, is revealed in Clinton Heylin's account in *Bob Dylan, Behind the Shades Revisited* (New York: HarperCollins, 2001), p. 187. For an account of the encounter and Dylan's contempt for "the forces *Time* and *Newsweek* represent," see W. Rothman, *Documentary Film Classics* (Cambridge: Cambridge University Press, 1997), pp. 189–193.

[2] According to Mike Marqusee, "Throughout the sixties, Dylan had seen himself as an uncompromising truth-teller, even when he was questioning assumptions about the very nature of truth." *Chimes of Freedom: The Politics of Bob Dylan's Art* (New York: The New Press, 2003), p. 270.

modern mass culture as an updated version of Plato's Cave[3] where unwitting subjects are fed a one-dimensional diet of man-ufactured reality. What role does the philosophical play in the development of Dylan's lyrical vision? How can philosophical reflection deepen appreciation of his contribution to our self-understanding? I don't think I can answer the first question, but in approaching it I hope to answer the second, showing how Dylan's imagination and craft bring philosophy to life, using poetry to make philosophical abstractions vivid and concrete.

It would be an exaggeration to describe this chapter as a philosophical study of the concept of 'truth' as found in Bob Dylan's work. Rather, Dylan's work is the point of departure as we look at two philosophical topics: (1) the idea that the "truth" consists of the correct correspondence of our subjective beliefs with an objective reality; and (2) our ability to use this standard of truth as we choose our own beliefs from a wide range of pos-sibilities. Today this is a critical problem: our culture of global communications confronts us with an overload of competing views and contrary belief systems. On a personal level, the same problem has always affected reflective individuals seeking answers to enduring questions of meaning and value in life. The appeal to philosophers of an artist such as Bob Dylan is directly related to the seriousness of his quest for the truth.

Nonetheless, "There are many here among us who feel that life is but a joke," as Dylan observes in "All Along the Watchtower." Perhaps, but experience has taught us otherwise: "But you and I, we've been through that, and this is not our fate." Yet this earnestness ("[s]o let us not talk falsely now") and urgency ("the hour is getting late") seem at odds with the alacrity with which he changes his beliefs. Does Dylan's history of changing com-mitments belie this seriousness? Examining the philosophical presuppositions of this question opens the door to a deeper dis-cussion of the nature of truth and belief.

---

[3] Plato's Cave refers to the "Allegory of the Cave" in Plato's *Republic VII*, where prisoners are bound and forced to look only at shadows cast on the cave wall. Without a point of comparison, the prisoners take the shadow reality as final and reject as "unserious" reports of one who had escaped the cave and returned with the truth. Socrates introduces this allegory with the statement, "Let me show in a figure how far our nature is enlightened or unenlightened." In *The Republic and Other Works* (New York: Doubleday Anchor, 1989), pp. 205–09.

"The Truth Is True Whether You Wanna Believe It or Not"[4]

Consider "The Lonesome Death of Hattie Carroll." Part reportage, part homily, the heart of this song is a narrative of an actual incident. The opening line baldly states the central fact of the tale: "William Zanzinger killed poor Hattie Carroll." There is no doubt that the singer believes this account is true. Belief is a matter of choice, but not so with truth. The truth of this line depends upon the facts, something independent of our wills. Some philosophers would explain that what it means to say that this statement is true is to say that William Zanzinger did indeed kill poor Hattie Carroll, and that the statement is true if, but only if, a corresponding fact exists in reality.[5]

Dylan himself advocates such a view of truth. In the notes to *Biograph* Dylan writes, "There does come a time, though, when you have to face facts and the truth is true whether you wanna believe it or not, it doesn't need you to make it true." The idea that "the truth is true whether you wanna believe it or not" is known as the objectivity of truth. But the more basic notion that "you have to face facts" is normative, which means that whether for moral or pragmatic reasons we ought to believe in the truth and ought not to believe what is false. Of course, we can always succumb to bad faith and put aside such norms of belief. As always, we may choose to do so or not. Nonetheless Dylan holds himself—and all of us—to a higher standard. Can we possibly abide by this standard?

Even if we agree with the austere doctrine that we have a duty to believe only the truth, we are still far from determining what the truth actually is with respect to the most important of life's questions. Should we choose a life of commitment and engagement or preserve an absolute freedom of choice, or at least some degree of autonomy? Likewise, Dylan pursues the

---

[4] *Biograph,* liner notes.
[5] This is often referred to as "the semantic theory of truth" following the formulation by the Polish logician, Alfred Tarski: "[A] true sentence is one which says that the state of affairs is so and so, and the state of affairs is indeed so and so." This is a version of "the correspondence theory of truth," which believes that a statement or belief is true if and only if it correctly corresponds to the facts. Alfred Tarski, *Logic, Semantics, Metamathematics, papers from 1923 to 1938,* second edition (Indianapolis: Hackett, 1983), p. 155.

question of whether we should seek our answers from a transcendent, higher order of reality, in other words God, or focus our thoughts on the immanent, the here and now. If we search through Dylan's work to find his answers to these questions, what we might see is a series of conflicting responses, open questions, and changes of mind. What is undeniable is Dylan's continuous willingness to change, sometimes to the great consternation of a public who would like to find in Dylan an affirmation of their own beliefs.

It is a commonplace to describe Dylan's career as a process of continuous reinvention. From New Left to counterculture to Christianity to Judaism and so on, Dylan continues to confound those who want to fix a label on his beliefs. However, it's clear that Dylan's beliefs have changed over time, and probably will continue to do so. (After all according to "It's Alright, Ma (I'm Only Bleeding)," "he not busy being born is busy dying.") Dylan's life and art, broadly viewed, present the paradox of strong conviction coupled with an openness to change. How does one preserve the right to grow in mind and spirit, changing beliefs over time ("stay forever young"), without implying that the truth is a matter of changing fashion?

Philosophical "relativism" addresses this question of change and multiplicity of beliefs. According to this view, the truth is not an unchanging and universal absolute, but rather something that might alter with history, vary among different cultures, or even change with the beliefs of each individual person. Perhaps the truth of one historical age differs from that of another (but only within that period). This is historical relativism. Or maybe truth is relative to a particular culture, society, or religion, so that the beliefs supported by one's culture are deemed true (but only within that culture). Or we might further relativize truth to the individual at a given point in time. This most radical form of relativism, often referred to as subjectivism, has a certain appeal particularly in our highly individualistic culture. To some, relativism seems a congenial, nonjudgmental form of liberality. In my experience it's almost a universal among undergraduates, and increasingly popular among so-called postmodern academic philosophers, who give up the notion of a transcendent point of view that might allow us to step out of our historical, cultural, or individual positions and see the truth simply. It is tempting, but wrong, to consider Dylan's continuously changing quest for the truth as evidence that he embraces this form of relativism.

You might think of relativism as a philosophic response to the bewildering diversity of thought and belief that our age of global communication has made inescapable. Moreover, it seems most democratic to extend toleration as widely as possible, and at the same time to avoid a theory of truth that would restrict its possession to any one absolute point of view. In another sense, relativism, in the form of subjectivism, would seem a proper philosophy for a culture and an age that values the freedom of individuals to choose their own belief systems. Again, one might see in relativism a defense of diversity against the domination of human thought by one point of view. The appeal of relativism as a theory of truth is reinforced by the difficulties associated with its alternative, often referred to as "absolutism."

Whereas a relativist might defend the idea of many truths— even among contrary beliefs—an absolutist will hold to the view that the truth is one and the same for all. Of course, the unavoidable consequence of this view is that when we encounter differences of belief we are compelled to admit the possibility that only one belief can be true, although many may be false. This might be understood merely as a matter of logic. Where two statements are contrary, for example, "My dog, Mr. Jones, is in St. Louis" and "My dog, Mr. Jones, is in Berkeley," at least one, and possibly both, statements must be false. And where statements are contradictory, for example, "my dog has fleas" and "my dog does not have fleas," if one is false the other is true. If we understand this to be a simple matter of logic, there is nothing inherently problematic with absolutism. Yet logic will drive us to understand that if my beliefs are true then contrary beliefs must be false. And this is what strikes many as not sufficiently open-minded. But the problem here does not lie with logic, but with the view that one side holds the absolute truth.

However, as we shall see where absolutism is held as merely a logical condition of the conflict of beliefs, and where no one belief is privileged, objections regarding tolerance and open-mindedness might be answered. To illustrate this point, consider the following lyric of "Precious Angel," from Dylan's first Christian album, *Slow Train Coming:*

> Ya either got faith or ya got unbelief and there ain't no neu-
>   tral ground
> The enemy is subtle, how be it we are so deceived
> When the truth's in our hearts and we still don't believe?

Here Dylan's thought is at its most absolutistic point: Christianity is the truth, and therefore any view at odds with it must be false. To maintain such a strong absolutist stance requires more than logic; there must be some basis for the claim to truth. Unfortunately, as we explain how we arrive at the truth, we must also explain how and why others fail to do so. For if the truth is actually "in our hearts" there must be a reason why "we still don't believe." And it is this explanation of error that causes problems. Herein lie the seeds of intolerance, where a difference of view-point is seen as an error and an error is seen as an evil, in this case the work of a subtle "enemy." Relativism seeks to avoid these consequences by denying that truth is absolute. Are there alternative solutions that preserve the logical point of absolutism, without denigrating the views of our doubters?

Searching for the Truth (the Way God Designed It)

> Lately I've been having evil dreams, I wake up in a cold blue
>   glare
> I run the tape back in my mind, wondering if I took the
>   wrong road somewhere
> Searching for the truth the way God designed it
> Well the real truth is that I may be afraid to find it ("Need a
>   Woman")[6]

The problem with absolutism, in the strong sense exemplified by Dylan's views in "Precious Angel" and elsewhere, is not just that it renders unnecessary any further search for the truth, but it

---

[6] The lyrics quoted here are unofficial and were accessed from http://hem .passagen.se/obrecht/backpages//Need A Woman. They are transcribed from the recording on *The Bootleg Series, volumes 1–3*. Regarding the problem of alternative versions of Dylan's songs, see Neal Corcoran, ed., *'Do You Mr. Jones?' Bob Dylan with the Poets and Professors* (London: Random House-Pimlico, 2003), pp.14–15.

denies the value of change. As Dylan sings elsewhere in *Slow Train Coming,* "Don't let me change my heart / Keep me set apart" ("I Believe in You"). Or, as he puts it in "Man in the Long Black Coat," "There are no mistakes in life some people say / It is true sometimes you can see it that way." Relativism has a similar drawback in its attitude to change. If every believer sets the standard by which to judge his or her own beliefs, or even if we simply deny the existence of some independent standard, it is difficult to understand how we can ever be in error. If the possibility of error is eliminated, there is little room for doubt and no need for change. It is the possibility of error, the admission of our fallibility, that makes the continued search for truth necessary. And without the idea of the truth as an objective standard or a norm ("the way God designed it"), the idea that we might have taken "the wrong road somewhere" would make little sense.

Dylan's journey is remarkable for its dramatic changes in philosophy. Often the changes are chronicled in transitional songs such as "My Back Pages," with its candid admission of error and its joy of self-discovery. The optimistic idea of a recovered youth that results when one casts off rigid ways of thinking ("lies that life is black and white") finds its most hopeful expression in "Forever Young," with its wish that one will "always know the truth." Not too far from this dream of a recovered, or even perpetual, youth is the spiritual utopia of a rebirth that comes upon achieving absolute truth. We have seen Dylan exploring this latter state of mind especially in the Christian albums. Yet the idea that he would remain within such an absolutist framework is hard to square with the general tendency of Dylan's work, which has long been informed by the sentiment that "he not busy being born is busy dying." And it's hardly surprising that in his later work we find dissatisfaction with the uncompromising absolutism of "Precious Angel" and similar songs of this period.

So we come back to the question: how can we claim truth is absolute and changeless, and yet remain open to change ourselves? Dylan's rejection of relativism, especially subjectivism, is emphatic: "That lie about everybody having their own truth inside of them has done a lot of damage and made people crazy."[7] So the resolution of these difficulties must preserve the idea of an objective truth.

---

[7] *Biograph,* liner notes.

The Blessings of Tranquility

Well I'm preachin' peace and harmony,
The blessings of tranquility ("Moonlight")

For Dylan, the truth is "that stuff that don't change,"[8] and his ever-changing and growing outlook exhibits a profound respect for this objective ideal of truth. Because of his respect for the truth, he is willing to change his own outlook to fit the truth as he finds it, rather than change the truth to suit himself. This can be broken down into three important ideas: (1) that the truth is a higher standard or ideal than our personal beliefs and preferences, but that (2) it remains always uncertain, and (3) that the pursuit of truth is a worthy, but ultimately open-ended, quest. The key idea is that because the truth is not ours to change and not always within reach, our beliefs at any time may be false.

The idea that the truth may be out of reach is known as skepticism. Many philosophers are apt to confuse this with relativism, but there is an important difference. Skeptics hold an idea of truth that is absolute but never fully assured. Therefore skeptics will advocate a suspension of judgment regarding the finality of one's beliefs. Whether one can actually live in accordance with a fully skeptical philosophy depends on whether this suspension of belief is equated with a paralyzing sense of doubt or with a healthy open-mindedness and rejection of dogma. (Dylan indicates his awareness of this danger when he refers to "strong men belittled by doubt" in "Where are You Tonight?") One ancient school of skepticism, the followers of Pyrrho of Elis (born around 365, died around. 270 B.C.E.), taught that such a suspense of judgment produces in the mind a sense of tranquility or unperturbedness. Skeptics who have surrendered to the idea that the quest for absolute truth is unending find themselves at peace with their uncertainty while able to continue to act and believe as they are naturally prompted to do: "I don't consider myself a sophist or a cynic or a stoic or some kind of bourgeois industrialist, or whatever titles people put on people."[9]

Dylan's disavowal of certain philosophical allegiances invites further study. Sophists, Cynics, and Stoics represent classical

---

[8] *Biograph*, liner notes.
[9] Mikal Gilmore, "Bob Dylan," *Rolling Stone* (22nd November, 2001), p. 64.

Greek and Roman philosophical positions with a direct relevance to our discussion. For example the most well-known of the Sophists was Protagoras (fifth century B.C.E.), who is credited with the earliest formulation of the relativist position, "Humans are the measure of all things." The Cynics, also dating to the fifth century B.C.E., were typified by Diogenes (born around 400, died around 325 B.C.E.), who claimed for himself the freedom of a dog, defying human customs and living without shame in a natural state. This philosophy is contemplated in the song "If Dogs Run Free" thusly: "Just do your thing, you'll be king / If dogs run free." But it was the Stoics who upheld an absolutist theory of truth, and who believed that tranquility can only be achieved by coming to absolute certainty regarding the truth and by living in accordance with the perfect plan of the universe.

Much of our knowledge of Stoicism comes from the *Meditations* of the Stoic Roman Emperor Marcus Aurelius (121–180 C.E.) who writes, "For all things throughout, there is but one and the same order; and through all things, one and the same God, the same substance and the same law. There is one common reason, and one common truth that belongs unto all reasonable creatures."[10] If he refuses the absolutist theory of the Stoics, and the relativistic theory of the Sophists, while rejecting the Cynics' attitude toward conventional human endeavor, what philosophical view might best enable us to understand Dylan's outlook consistently? I suggest we consider the views of the Pyrrhonian skeptics, who without rejecting the existence of objective truth deny the human ability to achieve it with certainty.

It is possible to trace a skeptical thread through Dylan's work, from the ambiguous refrain of one of his earliest works, "Blowin' in the Wind,"[11] to the world-weary admonition, "All the truth in the world adds up to one big lie" ("Things Have Changed"). Perhaps this might give us some clue regarding how we join an allegiance to absolute truth with an openness to change. It might also give us an insight into Dylan's most recent thinking, or at least a way to frame some of his later themes.

Among Dylan's most revealing songs is "Every Grain of Sand," the last cut on *Shot of Love*, which is the last of his so-

---

[10] Marcus Aurelius, *Meditations* (New York: Appleton, 1904), p. 74.
[11] Marqusee notes the "ambiguous" and "elusive" nature of the song's refrain: "The answer is blowin' in the wind," p. 55.

called Christian albums (preceded by *Slow Train Coming* and *Saved*). The quotes from the *Biograph* liner notes that I cited above regarding the objectivity of truth and the rejection of subjectivism were part of Dylan's comments on what he describes as "an inspired song." Although the song is intensely personal, Dylan's comments refer to its social background. Dylan characterizes it as decidedly out of step with its time, America in the early 1980s, which he called "the age of masturbation." As an antidote to this "crooked" age, Dylan appeals to "scripturally straight" values, "stuff that don't change." And there is a timelessness in this moving expression of uncertainty and faith. Dylan's words refer to this as "the hour of my deepest need," which is taken by some commentators as a confession of his uncertain faith.[12] There is clearly an honest admission of uncertainty in the climactic moment when he sings: "I hear the ancient footsteps like the motion of the sea / Sometimes I turn, there's someone there, other times it's only me" ("Every Grain of Sand").

Perhaps this gentle agnosticism explains the two different versions of the penultimate line of the song. In the studio recording, the lyric reads, "I am hanging in the balance of the reality of man," while on the home recording released on *The Bootleg Series, Volumes 1–3*, Dylan sings, "I am hanging in the balance of a perfect finished plan." One version echoes Protagoras, the other the Stoics. Both versions refer to "hanging in the balance," evoking the Pyrrhonian skeptical form of meditation where the evidence for belief is counterbalanced by contrary evidence until the mind finds a balance and achieves tranquility, as Sextus Empiricus describes in the passage below:

> Up to now we say that the aim of the sceptic is tranquility in matters of opinion and moderation of feeling in matters forced upon us. For Sceptics began to do philosophy in order to decide . . . which are true and which false, so as to become tranquil; but they came upon equipollent dispute [a dispute where arguments pro and con are balanced], and being unable to decide this they sus-

---

[12] Heylin, p. 529. For a dissenting view regarding the agnosticism of "Every Grain of Sand," see M. Gray, *Song and Dance Man III: The Art of Bob Dylan* (London: Cassell, 2000), p. 400ff.

pended judgement. Tranquility in matters of opinion followed for-tuitously.[13]

Dylan's most recent work develops the theme of a skeptical tranquility. In the 2000 single, "Things Have Changed," Dylan's attitude is "[o]nly a fool in here would think he's got anything to prove." Or contrast the early self-confident sentiments of "Subterranean Homesick Blues," "You don't need a weatherman / To know which way the wind blows" to the recent admission that "I'm not even acquainted with my own desires" ("Bye and Bye"). But it would be misleading to portray this as a new atti-tude of Dylan's. The clearest precursor is another, earlier single, "Watching the River Flow," where Dylan renounces confusion for a suspense of judgment ("People disagreeing on all just about everything, yeah / Makes you stop and all wonder why") and a life of tranquility: "I'll just sit here so contentedly / And watch the river flow." The river "keeps on rollin', though / No matter . . . which way the wind does blow," Dylan concludes. The river of time, the flow of facts, in reality remains unaffected by winds of belief, the flow of changing opinions. The same wise but noncommittal view is expressed in Dylan's aptly named "Floater" from *Love and Theft*, where the composer of "Blowin' in the Wind," "Idiot Wind," "Caribbean Wind," and oth-ers declares, "Sometimes it's just plain stupid / To get into any kind of wind."

Is there a comprehensive philosophical vision that would unify Dylan's art? Bryan Chevette has argued that the "constant restlessness and ambivalence" that has characterized his career is indicative of an underlying philosophy of sorts. This he explains is "a sense of absolute certainty in his own vision of continual and all-embracing uncertainty.[14] But I think it is a bit strong to attribute to Dylan any certainty at this philosophical level if we are to explain his embrace, even if provisional, of a faith believed to be absolutely true. And I think that any com-prehensive account of Dylan's philosophical journey needs also to come to terms with seriousness of his Christian absolutism. This is better explained by Dylan's consistent willingness to hold

---

[13] Sextus Empiricus, *Outlines of Scepticism* (Cambridge: Cambridge University Press, 1994), p. 10.
[14] "On the 'D' Train: Bob Dylan's Conversions," in Corcoran, p. 222.

even his uncertainty and ambivalence with less than certainty, rather than Chevette's paradoxical description of Dylan's uncertainty as an absolute. As Patrick Crotty claims, "Dylan approaches paradigmatic situations from so many angles and such a diversity of attitude that the paradigm can be missed or mistaken by the unwary."[15] Moreover, I think that accounts for the appearance of paradox. Dylan's challenge to his own uncertainty bespeaks an even deeper and more consistent philosophical position, which opens the door further to a Pyrrhonian interpretation of his attitude toward belief.

Sextus Empiricus contrasts his own Pyrhonnian brand of doubt with that of the competing school of Academic skeptics. The latter held their skeptical views dogmatically, as if to say that we can know for certain that there is no certain knowledge. Such a philosophy would fulfill Chevette's characterization of Dylan's position as "paradoxical." However, Sextus claims that Pyrhonnians do not dogmatize thus, rather they "utter their own phrases in such a way that they are implicitly cancelled by themselves, then they cannot be said to hold beliefs in uttering them." Sextus offers the statements "Nothing is true" or "All things are false" as examples of self-canceling phrases, rather than certainties.

Although I said at the outset that I would not attribute any philosophical views to Dylan, we can contemplate what such a philosophy would have to accomplish. I believe that would include a consistent way to maintain the ideal of objective truth as the standard of belief without denying uncertainty or the freedom to change one's mind. I would venture that the position outlined by Sextus provides us with one such view. In this way I hope to have shown how philosophical reflection deepens our appreciation for the universality of Dylan's art and how that art gives currency to perennial philosophical questions.

[15] "Bob Dylan's Last Words," in Corcoran, p. 325.

10

The Free Will in Bob Dylan

MARTIN VAN HEES

Davey Moore was a professional boxer who died after a fight against Sugar Ramos on March 21st, 1963. A few weeks after the match, Bob Dylan performed the song "Who Killed Davey Moore?" The song doesn't give a direct answer to the question its title poses. Rather, it lets those involved in the boxing match explain why they think they *can't* be held responsible for the young boxer's death. Take the referee, for instance. He argues that he was under pressure to continue the bout due to the interests at stake. The crowd only wanted to see a good fight. The manager claimed he didn't know that Moore wasn't physically up to the fight. The sports journalist and the gambler also deny any responsibility—the journalist thinks that boxing is a respectable American institution while the gambler argues that betting on the outcome of a match isn't the same as being responsible for what happens in it. So the referee, the public, the manager, the gambler, and the journalist all claim, "It wasn't me that made him fall."

So was it Sugar Ramos, Moore's opponent, who should be held responsible for the death? After all, Moore died from his punches. At the end of the song, Moore's opponent declares that he can't be held responsible, either. He was only doing his job: "I hit him, yes, it's true / But that's what I'm paid to do." And he adds, "Don't say 'murder,' don't say 'kill' / It was destiny, it was God's will."

"Who Killed Davey Moore?" is often taken as one of Dylan's early protest songs. It doesn't condemn boxing explicitly but implicitly—and that, in part, is what gives the song its impact. The song compels us to draw the conclusion that *all* those who support the existence of boxing matches share a responsibility, so they can all share the blame for Moore's death. As we listen we become convinced that the various arguments intended to exonerate the participants aren't so much untrue as *irrelevant.* Sure, the referee was under pressure; of course the crowd came to see a good fight, and so on and so forth. But none of them is exonerated by such considerations. Each and every one of them shares the responsibility for Moore's death. So as we listen we are drawn irresistibly to the conclusion that Ramos's statement is also true, and just as irrelevant. In other words, it was indeed destiny—God's will—but it was still a kill. The young boxer's death was inevitable, but it was no accident. Moore's death is something we must both mourn *and* condemn.

But *how* can people be responsible for their acts if fate reigns? The relation between fate, free will, and moral responsibility is a fundamental philosophical issue. It also plays an important role in Dylan's work, and, as we shall see, Dylan confronts it in a very sophisticated way.

Twisting Fate

According to some, the course of history is inevitable. Bob Dylan often refers to this inevitability as fate. We come across it in many Dylan songs. "Who Killed Davey Moore?" is just one of many of his songs in which fate brings about tragic events. The theme is sometimes depicted surrealistically ("A Hard Rain's A-Gonna Fall" or "Things Have Changed"), sometimes epically ("Blind Willie McTell"). Other songs go into great detail ("Ballad of Hollis Brown"). But it's always drawn vividly. "Ballad of Hollis Brown" evokes the desperation of a farmer and his family living in extreme poverty. His desperation leads the farmer to kill his wife, his five children, and himself. But this tragic event isn't the end of the song. The final lines push the song way beyond this particular family's horrible fate: "Somewhere in the distance / There's seven new people born."

Now, these lines don't rule out an optimistic interpretation, of course (along the lines of "new lives, new opportunities"). But the song's atmosphere is bleak and the music is repetitive, so it's clear that any such reading must be inappropriate. The opposite inference may even be suggested: there's not much we can do about such tragedies because they're part of nature's course. But that sort of pessimism is at most only part of the song's message. Above all, it's a song of protest. The vivid description of the farmer's misery allows us to feel the injustice of societies where people live in conditions like that. The closing line ("There's seven new people born") therefore reminds us that the injustice isn't just perpetrated on the Hollis Browns of the past, but also on all of those who are still living in extreme poverty. So, after evoking powerful feelings of injustice in us, caused by the vivid description of Hollis Brown's misery, Dylan's closing lines can be interpreted as an appeal to our own responsibility to bring about change.

But—and this is the paradox that the song shares with "Who Killed Davey Moore?"—how can we bear a responsibility for tragic events, if such events are inevitable? That is, how can we reconcile fate with the idea that people have a moral responsibility for their own actions?

This is a dilemma, and one way out of it is to say that the course of history is only partly fixed. Tragic events may occur; they're predestined to occur. But what's not fixed is *which* tragic events will occur, nor *how* they occur. Take Davey Moore's death once again: it could have been prevented if the match had been cancelled. Just as Hollis Brown's death and that of his family could have been prevented if they had received assistance. If that's true, then who let the match go ahead or who didn't offer assistance can be held responsible: we can blame them because they didn't intervene, even though their intervention wouldn't have stopped the deaths of other Davey Moores or Hollis Browns. Canceling one fight wouldn't stop other boxing deaths, which is what the journalist states when Dylan has him say: "[F]ist fighting is here to stay / It's just the old American way."

So the institution will still continue to claim victims.[1] But clearly, cancellation of the particular fight would have prevented the death of one *particular* boxer, Davey Moore. That may itself be sufficient to lay the blame on those involved.

---

[1] As of early 2004, more than three hundred ring deaths have followed Davey Moore's (J.R. Svinth, "Death under the Spotlight: The Manuel Velazquez Boxing Fatality Collection," *Journal of Combative Sports*, 2004).

Similarly, giving assistance to Hollis Brown wouldn't eradicate poverty in general—"There's seven new people born"—but it might have saved *his* life, and that of his family.

Even if it's true that history on the whole is fixed (there will still be prizefights, poverty will continue to exist), there may still be a possibility to make changes. You can't stop the river's current by throwing a pebble in, but—no matter how insignificantly—the pebble does affect the river's flow. Similarly, we may not be able to escape fate, but we may be able to give it a twist. So even if we can't prevent tragic events as such from occurring, we may share a responsibility for tragic events that do occur—and those that don't—in our own particular world. An awareness of the capabilities we have in this regard, even though they may be quite limited, is certainly part of what makes these songs protest songs.

Forces of Change

Let's call the view that allows for individuals to change particular events (but not the general course of things) the "Limited Optimistic View." But the early protest songs suggest an even more hopeful view of the human condition, which we'll call the "Expansive Optimistic View." On this view, individuals may not be able to make a very profound difference on their own, but if *all* of us throw pebbles into the river, its flow *can* be stopped—in theory, at least. This conviction doesn't belong exclusively to activists or to the ideology of past generations. On the contrary, to say that many can do more than a few is part of our conventional wisdom, not just the exclusive thought of revolutionaries. But it's not enough just to point out the possibility of such collective efforts, precisely because the difficulty of achieving them is also part of our conventional wisdom. If it's to be convincing or appealing, the prospect of joining forces collectively should also be irresistible. After all, if the forces leading to injustice are so strong as to seem part of the fate of mankind, they can only be overturned by forces that are even stronger. Since it is so difficult to achieve any joint effort to bring about such a change, the revolutionary's trick is to state its inevitability. Arguing for such huge changes would just highlight the difficulty of the task ahead—the forces of change would be seen as too weak to upset the forces of injustice.

So it's not surprising that two of the most influential songs of the 1960s—"Blowin' in the Wind" and "The Times They Are A-Changin'"—do not argue for change, they proclaim it. These anthems of the protest generation simply predict the demise of injustice. The announcement is implicit in "Blowin' in the Wind," while it's much more explicit in "The Times They Are A-Changin'." Things *will* be different: "The line is drawn / The curse is cast." The song doesn't ask us to man the barricades to help bring about a change (whatever that change may be); it just proclaims the change's inevitability.

Moreover—and this explains why the song had such a major social and political impact—since the change seems to be inevitable, you'd better be on the right side: "If your time to you is worth savin' / Then you better start swimmin' or you'll sink like a stone." The change will occur because people take the initiative to make change. And, paradoxically, they will take the initiative because they believe the change is inevitable. On this view, it's precisely the guarantee of the cause's success that gives the song its power.

Determinism

This broader perspective and the confidence these songs express now seem to be a typical feature of the optimism of the sixties, one that has lost credibility for many of us. Bob Dylan himself, of course, was one of the first to abandon this broad perspective. The famous words of "My Back Pages," in which he distances himself from his role as spokesperson of a new generation ("Ah, but I was so much older then / I'm younger than that now"), were recorded less than a year after "The Times They Are A-Changin'." Later on in his career, Dylan not only distanced himself further from his early optimism, but seems in fact to have become a full-blown pessimist. Our tragic fate can neither be influenced nor overcome. "Blind Willie McTell" is one example, perhaps the most powerful, most impressive evocation of a "Pessimistic View," one that denies humans the potentiality to alter any of the circumstances of their existence. Take the opening lines:

Seen the arrow on the doorpost
Saying, "This land is condemned

All the way from New Orleans
To Jerusalem"

It's not just the hope for Big Changes that is lost. Even the idea
that humans are responsible for making their own small changes
for the good now seems to have vanished. Tragic fate really has
got the upper hand now, and the possibility of affecting it seems
to have disappeared.

Some philosophers are reluctant to talk about "fate"; it has
too many theological connotations. But the idea that the course
of history is completely fixed has a long tradition among
philosophers. One of the main reasons for this theme's pre-
dominance within philosophy, of course, is that it elicits profound doubts about the possibility of moral responsibility. If
everything is predetermined—and therefore all the *particular*
actions adopted by *particular* individuals—then it is questionable whether we can be held responsible for our actions at all.
On this view, it's not only the existence of tragic events *as such*
that is predetermined. It's also predetermined that Davey Moore
and Hollis Brown would die, because all the individuals
involved could not have acted differently than they did. Take
the referee again: given the person he is, he could not have
acted any differently. He couldn't have stopped the fight. If we
were to attribute responsibility—at least *some* responsibility—to
him, where should we locate it? In his previous actions? In his
beliefs? But what if those beliefs and actions were in turn determined by earlier conditions (say his background or his previous
choices), which in turn were caused by yet earlier ones?

The thesis that every event or state of affairs is necessitated
by earlier events is called *determinism*. Preceding conditions
(which philosophers usually take to be laws of nature or laws
of logic, but they could just as well refer to God's will or fate)
dictate that only *that* particular event or state of affairs could
have obtained. It was inevitable since there is only one future.
In Dylan's words: "Well the future for me is already a thing of
the past" ("Bye and Bye").

Being Responsible in a Determinist World

The problem of reconciling moral responsibility with determinism has haunted philosophers for centuries and will undoubt-

edly continue to haunt them for many centuries to come. Some, though, say the problem is irrelevant simply because history's course is *not* predetermined—there's no such thing as destiny. Yet others take determinism to be true and try to bite the bullet. They deny the existence of moral responsibility, that is, they believe that since people cannot act differently than they do, they can't be held accountable for their actions. Both responses call forth new questions. Those who deny determinism (usually called "libertarians") should explain what it means to say that an act is non-determined and how such acts elicit responsibility. Those who deny responsibility (the so-called "hard determinists") should be able to explain how we can live in a meaningful way in a world where the idea of responsibility is absent.

There is a philosophical stance that takes the middle ground between these two extremes, the position of the "compatibilists." They argue that there is no inherent tension between responsibility and determinism. The two are compatible. The philosopher Harry Frankfurt has famously proposed a defense of compatibilism based on the argument that moral responsibility does not presuppose the possibility of acting differently.[2] A person can be held responsible for an action yet need not have been able to act differently. On this view, the crucial point for attributing responsibility isn't whether the person could have done otherwise, but whether or not he condoned the action. Did he willingly perform the action that co-determined the tragic event, or did he deplore that action but lacked an alternative possibility? One of the most widely discussed arguments in contemporary philosophy goes like this: Suppose a person— Jones, say—is planning to perform some action. Without his knowing, another person—Black—has implanted some fancy control mechanism in Jones's brain. Black very much wants Jones to perform *x*, and he would certainly intervene and use his mechanism if Jones were to hesitate about the action. Now

---

[2] Harry Frankfurt, "Alternate Possibilities and Moral Responsibility," reprinted in *The Importance of What We Care About: Philosophical Essays* (Cambridge: Cambridge University Press, 1988), pp. 1–10. The essay is also reprinted in David Widerker and Michael McKenna, ed., *Moral Responsibility and Alternative Possibilities: Essays on the Importance of Alternative Possibilities* (Aldershot: Ashgate, 2003), which forms a collection of recent essays on Frankfurt's argument.

suppose that Jones, *for reasons of his own*, performs *x*. Given this, there's no need for Black to intervene: it really is Jones's decision to perform the act.

In such situations, Frankfurt argues, we will say that Jones is responsible for his actions, even though it's true that he couldn't have acted any differently. After all, if he had hesitated, Black would have intervened so that Jones would have performed the action in any case. It's therefore not necessary to have alternative options open to you in order for you to be responsible for your actions. Insofar as the possible tension between determinism and responsibility hinges on the idea that determinism implies the absence of alternative options, then the tension disappears.

Moral Autonomy

To return to Davey Moore, we see that all those involved in the boxing match do indeed consent to the match. In giving their reasons, the manager, the journalist, and the boxers themselves all make clear that they agreed to the match being fought. This explains why they can be held responsible and why Dylan's song can be labeled a protest song. It protests against those who endorse an event in which people can die, and it thus appeals to us to refrain from supporting such events.

Similarly, we are responsible for the misery of all Hollis Browns if we consent to that misery's existence—even though we may not be able to change it. The circumstances under which our consent assigns responsibility to us—which reasons we really call "our own"—is a difficult philosophical question that we won't go into here. But *that*, even in a fully determined world, our consent constitutes responsibility is a point of view that Bob Dylan shares with the compatibilists. Indeed, the desirability of taking such a stance is a conviction that Dylan never abandoned, either in his life or his work. This desire for what we may label *moral autonomy* in a world where fate reigns, finds perhaps its most beautiful rendition in the chilling last verse of "Blind Willie McTell." (Although I hasten to add that this is only one of many possible ways to interpret these lines.)

Well, God is in heaven
And we all want what's his

But power and greed and corruptible seed
Seem to be all that there is
I'm gazing out the window
Of the St. James Hotel
And I know no one can sing the blues
Like Blind Willie McTell

From the bleak outlook of fate and our inability to change things ("seem to be all that there is"), the first part of this verse implies that we're condemned to the role of a spectator ("I'm gazing out the window"). But, just like the old blues singers did, there is the possibility of describing and lamenting our fate. This in itself equates to taking a stance. Achieving this ideal may be very difficult—even impossible for some ("And I know no one can sing the blues / Like Blind Willie McTell"). So it's no easy thing for us to take up our moral responsibility, but the idea that we can and should strive to do so, even in a world where we are merely "pawns in a game," forms the essence of our moral autonomy.[3]

[3] For their helpful comments I would like to thank the editors of this volume, Jasper Caarls, Katherine Gardiner, Miran Huizenga, and Ian Priestnall.

11

"I Got My Bob Dylan Mask On": Bob Dylan and Personal Identity

PETER VERNEZZE and PAUL LULEWICZ

Most people believe they are the same person from birth to death. Philosophers have a field day exposing the weaknesses in their justifications for this position. So does Bob Dylan. It shouldn't surprise us, then, that Dylan's art and life can serve as an entryway into the problem of personal identity.

The Mask of Zimmerman

The quote in our chapter title comes from Dylan's October 31st, 1964, concert at Carnegie Hall. During some banter with the audience Dylan remarked: "It's Halloween. I got my Bob Dylan mask on."[1] The audience laughed, but it's worth probing the implications of the statement.

To say that someone is wearing a mask of a living person is to say (obviously) that one is not that person. If you are wearing a Dick Cheney mask in order to scare your friends, it means you are not Dick Cheney. But what does it mean to have the person headlining the October 31st concert at Carnegie Hall announce that he's wearing a "Bob Dylan" mask? It implies at least that the person speaking is not Bob Dylan. The statement is puzzling precisely because we assume that the person making the statement is Bob Dylan. But if Bob Dylan is not Bob Dylan, who is?

Tackling this issue will require a philosophical investigation into the topic of personal identity. Most of us identify with some aspect of ourselves. We become our jobs, for instance, or define

---

[1] *The Bootleg Series, Volume 6: Live 1964.*

ourselves by our roles as parents and spouses. But is that who we really are? This is not quite the personal identity question, which asks not what makes us essentially who we are but, to be precise, what justifies us in claiming that a person who exists at one time is identical with a person (or anything for that matter) that exists at another time. But clearly, answering the first question will be relevant to answering the personal identity question, for claiming that we are the same person at two different times assumes that there is something that identifies me as me. Here, we'll concern ourselves with the personal identity issue and bring in Bob Dylan to help explore the various ways that philosophers have tried to answer the question, "What is it in virtue of which we can claim to be the same person at different times?"

Who Is Bob Dylan?

Born Robert Allen Zimmerman in Duluth, Minnesota, on May 24th, 1941, Bob Dylan grew up a short distance away in Hibbing. Is Bob Dylan Robert Zimmerman? Now we begin to ask the personal identity question. What makes the performer in 1964 identical with the young man whose family moved to Hibbing, Minnesota, in 1946? One answer is that Bob Dylan is the same person in 1964 as in 1946 and in 2006 because he has the same body. Let's call this the "physicalist" view of personal identity: What makes a person the same at different times are his physical constituents. Now obviously, our bodies are in flux. We entirely replace the majority of our internal cells every seven years; we are born small and grow large; our hair turns grey, or falls out. "Everything is in flux" applies to nothing more than to the human body—and Dylan's voice. But despite innumerable fluctuations, we can identify a causal relationship between our bodies at various points in our lives that allows us to claim coherently that it is the same body over time. The "same body, same person" principle supplies an easy answer to the question of who Bob Dylan, or anyone, is. The physical body performing at Carnegie Hall in 1964 is causally connected to the body born in St. Paul in 1946. One and the same living organism will have generated any changes.

But does the same body make the same person? Suppose that in the early 1980s Dylan's brain had been transplanted into the body of a Christian evangelist and that this evangelist's brain had been placed in Dylan's body, which was on tour convincing people that it had become born again. Under these circumstances, I think we would want to say that the person performing on stage was not Bob Dylan. Indeed if anything were to count as Bob Dylan, it would be the entity in possession of Dylan's brain. Most of us share the same intuition about brain transplant scenarios. That is, we believe that if our brain were placed in another body, the body with our brain would be us regardless of how it looked, so long as it continued to have our memory and personality. Why not, then, identify the self with the brain or some part of the brain, perhaps the cerebrum? This might seem to save the physicalist account, since the cerebrum would appear to be a physical criterion for the self. But the reason we would identify the entity with Dylan's cerebrum as Dylan is not because it contains a particular lump of his physical matter but because of the presence of certain mental traits such as memory and personality. But then we are no longer identifying an individual with his physical constituents but with some set of psychological traits. Hence, we will turn to examine one of the most prominent of the psychological answers to what constitutes the self.

"I'll Remember You"

Despite its intuitive appeal, the view that we can be identified with our body faces a rather compelling counterexample. A much more promising account of what constitutes personal identity was put forward by John Locke (1632–1704), perhaps the first philosopher to worry seriously about the issue of what makes us the same person across time. Locke's view is best understood as claiming that it is my memory that identifies me as the same person across time. That is, I am the same person as someone from an earlier period if I have a consciousness or memory of myself as that person. In his *Essay Concerning Human Understanding*, Locke wrote: "In this alone consists personal identity, i.e., the sameness of a rational being; and as far as this consciousness can be extended backwards to any past action or thought, so far reaches the identity of that person."[2]

---

[2] In John Perry, ed., *Personal Identity* (Berkeley: University of California Press, 1975), p. 39.

This position, which we will call the "memory view," has no trouble handling the brain transplant counterexamples. According to the memory view, the Christian evangelist with Dylan's brain who was performing religious tunes on stage in the early 1980s would not have been Bob Dylan because he would not have had the memories of being Bob Dylan, would not recall, for instance, being booed off the stage at the 1964 Newport Folk Festival (yes, we realize there is debate about what exactly happened there). One implication of the memory view that will interest us here is that if it is the persistence of memory that makes me who I am, then there is nothing theoretically to bar me from being the same person from an earlier historical period. Locke accepts this implication.

> [W]hatever has the same consciousness of present and past actions, is the same person to whom they both belong. Had I the same consciousness that I saw the ark and Noah's flood, as that I saw an overflowing of the Thames last winter, or as that I write now; I could no more doubt that I who write this now, that saw the Thames overflowed last winter, and that viewed the flood at the general deluge, was the same self, place that self in what substance you please, than that I who write this am the same myself now whilst I write . . . that I was yesterday.[3]

The scenario of possible past lives provides a good way to evaluate Dylan's connection to the memory view. The position that the same self can exist across several lifetimes gets an airing in some of Dylan's lyrics. "Shelter from the Storm" begins with what sounds like an account of a previous existence: "'Twas in another lifetime, one of toil and blood / When blackness was a virtue and the road was full of mud." Although Dylan may be speaking metaphorically here, "Oh Sister" relates a tale of two characters who "died and were reborn." Likewise "I and I" finds the singer with a strange woman who, "In another lifetime . . . must have owned the world or been faithfully wed / To some righteous king who wrote songs besides moonlight streams."

Although there are several references to past lifetimes and previous existences, it doesn't seem the issue of memory is cen-

---

[3] Perry, *Personal Identity*, p. 45.

tral to the concept of the identity of the self across time in these situations. True, in "Shelter from the Storm" the narrator retains specific memories, for example, that someone removed a crown of thorns from his head. But in "Oh Sister" the situation is much more ambiguous. The assertion that "[w]e grew up together from the cradle from the grave" lacks the specificity of memory and may be nothing more than an unfounded belief of the song's narrator. "I and I" provides no evidence that the woman herself retains the memories of owning the world or being married to a king in a previous life. It seems that sometimes the characters do have memories of a previous existence, sometimes they don't, and sometimes we just can't tell. Hence the notion of memory is not essential to Dylan's view of the identity of the self, since he is willing to assert the identity of the self across several lifetimes without really being concerned about whether that self retains any memory of these lives.

In these lyrics of reincarnation Dylan does not seem to ascribe to the memory view of personal identity and it's just as well, for the theory is not without its problems. Consider the following. Suppose that the performer on stage in 1964 remembers being a young boy in Minnesota. Flash ahead to an eighty-year-old Bob Dylan (still touring, thankfully) who recollects his performance in 1964 but has no memory of his childhood. According to Locke's memory view, the performer in 1964 is the same person as the young boy in Minnesota (because he has consciousness of being that person), and the octogenarian is the same person as the performer in 1964. But then the eighty-year-old Dylan is not the same person as the young boy in Minnesota, which violates the basic logical tenet of identity: If A = B and B = C, then A = C.[4]

This is only the beginning of the difficulties for the memory view, which has had more than its share of critics and defenders since it was first proposed in the seventeenth century. We do not intend to examine the history of this controversy here, but it is perhaps worth laying out a few more issues. Our memories are at best sporadic and incomplete so that it seems there are many parts of our own life that we will not be connected with

---

[4] This criticism of the memory view is given by Thomas Reid, "Of Mr. Locke's Account of Our Personal Identity," in Perry, p. 113–18.

by this theory of personal identity. And consider the case of Alzheimer's disease. If my uncle has no recollection of his past, then according to the memory view he would not be the same person as the one who, for example, took me fishing as a child. Hence, my ethical duty to visit him in a nursing home would be no stronger than it would be to visit any other patient there. But clearly I have some special obligation to my uncle that I do not have to other patients in the nursing home. According to the memory view, however, it is hard to explain what that obligation is. It is difficulties like these that might lead one to consider a third theory of personal identity, one that with more certainty can be attributed to Dylan for at least part of his career.

A Soul Man?

One of the most common accounts of personal identity, at least in the Christian West, is the belief that what makes me the same person across time is neither my body nor my memory but my soul. According to this view, the soul is understood as a non-physical entity that is attached to a particular body. Though this soul is separate from the body, it is generally held to come into existence at roughly the same time as the body, remain with the body over the course of a single life and, finally, face judgment for eternity as a result of its actions on this earth. On this way of looking at things, what makes the person born Robert Zimmerman the same person as the performer known as Bob Dylan is the persistence of the same soul. This view has a more limited following among philosophers than laypersons, but it is not without its contemporary defenders and an impressive pedigree. Plato hypothesized the existence of a non-physical entity that is subject to reward and punishment in an afterlife. And famously René ("I think, therefore I am") Descartes, after he had undermined his ground for belief in almost everything, could not doubt the existence of an immaterial substance—a non-physical self—that constituted his essence.

In the albums associated with his conversion to Christianity (*Slow Train Coming, Saved, Shot of Love*) Dylan clearly adopted a viewpoint that we are in possession of an eternal soul, one that will be accountable in the afterlife for its actions on this earth. In "When He Returns," Dylan announces that Christ has "plans to set up his throne / When He returns." As Revelation

20:11–15 (which the lyrics are alluding to) makes clear, during this period the dead will be "judged according to their deeds" and those who fall short will be "thrown into the pool of fire." Here, then, Dylan is announcing his assent to a scenario that involves retribution for individual eternal souls. Along the same lines, Dylan speaks in "Precious Angel" of a time when "men will beg God to kill them and they won't be able to die." They will beg God to kill them, obviously, because their soul has been condemned to Hell, and they do not wish to suffer such punishment for eternity. Indeed, it is the existence of this soul that explains why it doesn't matter whether you call him Bobby or Zimmy ("Gotta Serve Somebody"). What you call him (or what he calls himself) is irrelevant, since his eternal soul will be judged by whom it serves regardless of what name it is referred to on this earth.

The Christian viewpoint involves a very definite take on the personal identity problem, one that can in fact respond to the shortcomings we found in the physicalist view and the memory view. For example, the concern about brain transplants that stymied the physicalist account can be handled by connecting the soul with the brain so that the body that gets my brain will also receive my soul and (in accord with our sentiments about the issue) be me as well. Descartes, who placed the soul in the brain's pineal gland, would be perfectly content with this outcome. Concerns about gaps in or the complete failure of memory need not trouble the soul view of personal identity, since the persistence of the soul will guarantee the continued existence of the self. But a myriad of difficulties await the soul view as well.

For one, we need to ask how we can claim to know that the soul exists. Adherents of the soul view must assume the presence of a body automatically entails the existence of a corresponding soul. But suppose you're offered a box of chocolates. Since you really like coconut fillings, you choose one that is swirled in a particular way because you know from past experience that chocolates swirled in this way contain coconut fillings. That is, you assume "same swirl outside, same filling inside." But the only reason you can know that there is coconut filling on the inside is because in the past you have experienced coconut filling in conjunction with that particular swirl. If you had never experienced that swirl with that filling, you would not now be able to know that the chocolate had coconut inside. But since we have never had the experience of the soul (but only of the body), our assumption that the soul exists inside the body cannot be said to be justified.[5] And even if for the sake of argument we grant the existence of a soul, how do we know that it is the same soul that exists over the course of a lifetime? Clearly, there is nothing impossible in assuming that a person receives a new soul every five years—or every five minutes—and that this soul takes over all of the memories of the one it is replacing.[6] So the soul view, although undoubtedly accepted by Dylan for at least a part of his career, faces major problems.

"Nobody's Bob Dylan"

We have surveyed versions of the three main accounts of personal identity: the notion that personal identity is constituted by a physical component (the body), a psychological trait (our memory of ourselves across time), and by a spiritual reality (an eternal soul). Each faces a rather substantial hurdle. Perhaps we should conclude that there is no permanent self that constitutes our personal identity. This is the position of the great Scottish philosopher David Hume (1711–1766). For Hume, the notion that there exists a self—something that is permanent and stable and can identify us across time—is an illusion. Instead of a single fixed entity at our core, what we find when we examine ourselves are isolated perceptions that are themselves subject to change. At this moment I have a particular impression (this computer screen), am possessed of a distinct emotion (anxiety about the chapter I am writing), reflect on a specific memory (what I had for breakfast), and call up a long-standing belief (that Dylan is a great poet). But in the next moment, I will be staring not at the computer screen but out the window, unconcerned with the paper, remembering a dinner two days ago, and perhaps (just perhaps) beginning to wonder if albums like *Knocked Out Loaded* and *Down in the Groove* are not enough to call into question Dylan's genius. What I thought I could appeal to as a source of stability and a ground for the self is, Hume claims,

---

[5] John Perry, *Dialogue on Personal Identity and Immortality* (Indianapolis: Hackett, 1979), p. 15.
[6] Perry, *Dialogue*, pp. 16–17.

subject to change. We are, according to Hume, "nothing but a bundle or collection of different perceptions, which succeed each other with an inconceivable rapidity, and are in a perpetual flux and movement."[7]

Although such a view may sound simply bizarre or incomprehensible to many in the West, the notion that there is no self lies at the core of Buddhism. According to the teaching of the Buddha, "The idea of the self is an imaginary, false belief which has no corresponding reality."[8] The Buddhist view is that what we refer to as the self is in fact a bundle of five aggregates: matter, sensations, perceptions, mental formations, and consciousness. Since these collections are themselves the result of causes and subject to constant change, what we call the self has no more permanence than a flame that is passed from one candle to the next.

The physicalist view, the memory view, and the soul view each sits rather comfortably with the conventional sense that we have a static, fixed essence. By contrast, the Buddhist-Humean view of the self overturns our conceptions of ourselves as stable beings with a solid identity. Where do Dylan's sentiments lie on this issue? We'd like to conclude with some thoughts that suggest Dylan is not without sympathy for the no-self view. Dylan himself seems to ascribe to a version of this view when he states in a relatively recent interview: "I mean, I think one thing today and I think another thing tomorrow. I change during the course of a day. I wake and I'm one person, and when I go to sleep I know for certain I'm somebody else. I don't know *who* I am most of the time."[9] Nor should we view this metaphysical musing as an isolated incident, for other evidence can be brought in to support its odd implication. The fact that the very name "Bob Dylan" is a construct, a fabrication, ought to alert us that Dylan may well be out to call into question our conceptions about identity. "Nobody's Bob Dylan. Bobby Dylan's long gone," says Dylan in an interview with Allen Ginsberg.[10]

---

[7] David Hume, "On Personal Identity," in Perry, *Personal Identity*, p. 162.

[8] Walpola Rahula, *What the Buddha Taught* (New York: Grove, 1972), p. 79.

[9] Quoted in Benjamin Hedin, ed., *Studio A: The Bob Dylan Reader*, (New York: Norton, 2004), p. 236.

[10] Stephen Scobie, *Alias Bob Dylan Revisited* (Calgary: Red Deer Press, 2003), p. 45.

The notion that there is such a thing as the artist Bob Dylan, an individual performer whose essence we can fix in time and space, is undercut by the many permutations that Dylan himself has undergone in his career—from protest singer to electric guitar rock star to country gentleman to Christian evangelist to folk archivist to whatever the latest permutation might be. It's hard to think of anyone more fluid as a performer than Dylan. The ever-shifting nature of the artist might help to explain the enigmatic comment: "I don't think of myself as Bob Dylan. It's like Rimbaud said, 'I is another'."[11]

One sense in which Dylan might be "another" is suggested by the Buddhist view of ego. Buddhists ground their argument that there is no self on the doctrine of causation, the notion that nothing can have the sort of essence required to be a truly separate being because everything is the product of causes. An individual enters the world possessed of a given set of genetic traits, grows up in a distinct family situation which is embedded in a particular culture at a certain place and time—none of which she is responsible for and all of which goes into determining her peculiar make up. Such a scenario, it is claimed, undermines the justification for belief in a self-caused essence. In the same way, by spending much of the past ten years recording the music of others, or by titling an album which consists mainly of covers *Self Portrait,* Dylan himself seems to be calling attention to the fact that the very musical genius we identify with him may be nothing more than a link in a chain, the result of countless other performers and traditions. Under such conditions, perhaps the creator does not warrant being distinguished as a fixed, self-created essence in his own right; rather, it is the chain that is the fundamental reality.[12]

---

[11] *Biograph,* liner notes.
[12] We would like to thank William Larkin for his helpful comments on this chapter.

12

With God (and Socrates and Augustine) on Our Side

JAMES S. SPIEGEL

The world of Dylan's songs features an endless cast of characters, from one-eyed midgets and jelly-faced women to Willie McTell and Charles Darwin. But the one constant presence—sometimes appearing on stage but usually looming behind the curtain—is God. Prior to 1967, Dylan's references to the divine were scant and mostly playful. His fabled motorcycle accident in Woodstock changed that. This event simultaneously signaled the end of Dylan's beat poet period and introduced a moral-spiritual seriousness to his lyrics that has never waned. If Dylan was always an American cultural prophet, this tag has been more literally applicable since *John Wesley Harding*. Whether speaking of, to, for, or about God, the post-accident Dylan is consistently God-concerned.

For the most part Dylan's music is colored by faith, rather than obsessed with it. His (in)famous gospel phase, from 1979 to 1981, is an exception, of course. But the self-righteousness and theological dogma of that period eventually settled into the brand of faith that characterizes most believers—a continuing quest to make sense of God and an anxious hope for life beyond the grave. Dylan's once bold proclamations have been tempered by life's fits and storms, but his reliance on God for salvation remains unshaken. Occasionally, Dylan still offers spiritual counsel, as on the closing line of *"Love and Theft"*: "Look up, look up—seek your Maker—'fore Gabriel blows his horn." But the attitude is less insistent, the posture more humble.

The combination of Dylan's religiosity and analytical nature would suggest that there is philosophical food for thought in his music about various issues in philosophy of religion. Indeed there is, and some of the recurrent themes are divine providence, original sin, and human immortality.

Every Grain of Sand

A theist is someone who believes in a personal, almighty, and perfectly good God. Theists also maintain that God governs the universe, which is the doctrine of providence—God "provides" for human beings and the rest of creation. But theists disagree about what this provision entails. The oldest tradition, dating back to Augustine (354–430), sees divine providence as comprehensive, covering even the smallest details of history, including human choices. Thus, Aquinas: "All things are subject to divine providence, not only in general, but in their own individual selves . . . all things that exist in whatsoever manner are necessarily directed by God towards some end."[1]

This is the *strong* view of divine providence. Other theists, especially in more recent times, have opted for a looser conception, where God governs the cosmos with a degree of passivity. God actively controls some events, like when parting the Red Sea, but he simply permits certain other events, such as human actions. Explains David Basinger: "To the extent that God grants individuals freedom, he gives up complete control over the decisions that are made." So "God, in a very real sense, [is] a *risk-taker*."[2] This is the *weak* view of providence.

Both views of divine providence appear in Dylan's songs. In some cases, God appears as essentially one more—if especially powerful—player on the world's stage:

> Oh God said to Abraham, "Kill me a son"
> Abe says, "Man, you must be puttin' me on"
> God say, "No." Abe say, "What?"

---

[1] Thomas Aquinas, *Summa Theologiae*, 1.Q22, A2, three volumes (New York: Benziger Brothers, 1947), 1:122.
[2] David Basinger, *The Case for Freewill Theism* (Downers Grove: InterVarsity Press, 1996), p. 33.

God say, "You can do what you want, Abe, but
The next time you see me comin' you better run"
Well Abe says, "Where do you want this killin' done?"
God says, "Out on Highway 61" ("Highway 61 Revisited")

This goofy, near-blasphemous rendering of the *Genesis* 22 narrative is definitely weak providence stuff. There is no doubt that God is in charge—just look at Abe's response—but he uses persuasion (or is it blackmail?), appealing to poor Abe's free will rather than moving him around like a marionette. Fortunately for the latter, not to mention the whole nation of Israel, the great patriarch played along. God took a risk, and Abe took the bait.

Here's another illustration of the weak view of providence, this time in a more serious song-context:

The sun turned cold over President Street and the town of
    Brooklyn mourned
They said a mass in the old church near the house where he
    was born
And someday if God's in heaven overlookin' His preserve
I know the men that shot him down will get what they
    deserve ("Joey")

In these cases, God's interaction with the world seems exceptional, a deviation from divine routine. Typically, he lets things run on their own, allows humans to behave as they will, that is until some grave injustice has been done (such as the killing of an innocent man) or God has some special plan he wants carried out (such as the killing of an innocent man). On the weak view of providence, God's control is general and open rather than meticulous, a matter of containment rather than unilateral dictation.

A much stronger view of providence emerges in most other Dylan songs where God appears. During the gospel period, Dylan declared God's plan for the world to be both unilateral—

Of every earthly plan that be known to man, He is uncon-
    cerned
He's got plans of His own to set up His throne
When He returns ("When He Returns")

and meticulous—

> In the fury of the moment I can see the Master's hand
> In every leaf that trembles, in every grain of sand ("Every
>   Grain of Sand")

And in some songs (such as "What Can I Do for You?" and "Ring Them Bells") an Augustinian (sometimes known as "Calvinist") view of predestination emerges. Dylan regards himself as one of the "chosen few," his salvation ultimately a consequence of God's choice, not his own.

The strong view of providence affirms divine sovereignty over even human free will. This view is known as theological determinism. But doesn't that negate human freedom? Not at all, they claim; the two are quite compatible. Thus, those who believe in both determinism *and* human freedom are called *compatibilists*. A person is free, on this view, just so long as she can *act* according to her choice, even though that choice is caused by pre-existing conditions, whether psychological factors (such as desires, fears, etc.) or divine decrees. Thus, Augustine writes: "We are by no means compelled, either, retaining the prescience of God, to take away the freedom of the will, or, retaining the freedom of the will, to deny that He is prescient of future things, which is impious. But we embrace both. We faithfully and sincerely confess both. The former, that we may believe well; the latter, that we may live well."[3]

So granting God's complete control over the entire cosmos, including human wills, does not preclude real freedom, says the compatibilist. The salient question is not whether a person's will is determined but whether she can act in accordance with her will. To be able to do as one pleases is to be free.

Defenders of weak providence take a different approach, preferring to understand human freedom as a lack of complete determination of the will. As Alvin Plantinga defines it, an action is free for a person if "it is within his power, at the time in question, to take or perform the action and within his power to refrain from it."[4]

---

[3] Augustine, *The City of God*, 1.5.10, trans. Marcus Dods (New York: Hafner, 1948), p. 196.

[4] Alvin Plantinga, *God, Freedom, and Evil* (Evanston: Harper and Row, 1974), p. 29.

So a person is free if and only if she really can choose, say, to buy or not to buy Dylan's *Self Portrait* album. This is known as the *power of contrary choice*. If, other conditions being the same, she could have purchased or refrained from purchasing *Self Portrait* (the latter being the wise choice in this case, of course), then her choice was free. Otherwise, it was not. This is known as a *libertarian* conception of freedom. Understandably, libertarians are drawn to a weak conception of providence because it preserves the power of contrary choice.

Dylan's lyrics typically illustrate a compatibilist approach, affirming both strong providence and human responsibility. Dylan's renowned moral judgmentalism (which assumes both freedom and responsibility) pervades his entire musical catalogue, most pronounced in such seething classics as "Masters of War," "Positively 4th Street," "Idiot Wind," and "When You Gonna Wake Up?" Combine this with theological determinism, and you have compatibilism. But Dylan sometimes goes even further, explicitly denying libertarian power of contrary choice:

> There's a whole lot of hearts breaking tonight
> From the disease of conceit
> Whole lot of hearts shaking tonight
> From the disease of conceit
> Steps into your room
> Eats your soul
> Over your senses
> You have no control
> Ain't nothing too discreet
> About the disease of conceit ("Disease of Conceit")

> Temptation's not an easy thing, Adam given the devil reign
> Because he sinned I got no choice, it run in my vein
>   ("Pressing On")

But, the libertarian asks, how can we be culpable for sin when we have "got no choice"? What freedom is possible when we "have no control"? This is the conundrum that plagues compatibilism. And precisely for this reason, some opt for *hard determinism*, which denies that human beings really are free in any significant sense. But advocates of strong providence—at least those who are classical theists—believe in human moral responsibility. So that's not a live option. Consequently, many appeal to theological mystery. But most prefer to stick to their guns, emphasizing their definition of freedom as acting according to one's choices (as opposed to exercising the power of contrary choice). They say the inability to control one's will does not preclude freedom. Though I suffer from the "disease of conceit" and sin "run[s] in my vein," the actions that follow from my moral sickness are still genuinely *my* actions. Therefore, I am culpable for them.

Ain't No Man Righteous

In philosophical theology, as in all branches of philosophy, there are no doctrinal islands. One's perspective on providence is vitally connected to one's other views. None are more pivotal here than the doctrine of human nature. Dylan's songs illustrate this. The theme of human depravity recurs in his music, dating back to his early folk days. But since the late seventies Dylan's indictments of human nature have been fervent and frequent. In "Man in the Long Black Coat" he says that "every man's conscience is vile and depraved." Elsewhere he adds:

> I was blinded by the devil
> Born already ruined
> Stone-cold dead
> As I stepped out of the womb ("Saved")

> Uttering idle words from a reprobate mind
> Clinging to strange promises, dying on the vine
> Never being able to separate the good from the bad
> Dead man, dead man
> When will you arise?
> Cobwebs in your mind
> Dust upon your eyes ("Dead Man, Dead Man")

Perhaps part of the intuitive appeal that Dylan finds in Christian theology is its concept of original sin. First articulated by Augustine in the fourth century, this is the doctrine that human beings suffer from an innate moral corruption. When our foreparents, Adam and Eve, rebelled against God, all of their progeny "fell" with them, inheriting their guilty status before God because they were our representative heads. But original sin is more than the mere forensic status of *guilt*; it is also moral *pollution*. Thus, we suffer from a natural rebellious tendency, shown in the sorts of pride, selfishness, and vanity to which Dylan repeatedly refers:

> Now he worships at an altar of a stagnant pool
> And when he sees his reflection, he's fulfilled
> Oh, man is opposed to fair play
> He wants it all and he wants it his way ("License to Kill")

> Well, God is in heaven
> And we all want what's his
> But power and greed and corruptible seed
> Seem to be all that there is ("Blind Willie McTell")

Augustine asserts that "two penalties—ignorance and difficulty—beset every sinful soul. Through ignorance, the soul is disgraced by error. Through difficulty, it is tormented by pain."[5]

The first penalty, sometimes called the "noetic effects of sin," appears in our inclination to err in our beliefs, to think the wrong things. Human judgment is basically distorted, and even our most profound insights prove deceptive. In Dylan's words,

> Soon as a man is born, you know the sparks begin to fly
> He gets wise in his own eyes and he's made to believe a lie
>   ("What Can I Do for You?")

> Now he's hell-bent for destruction, he's afraid and confused
> And his brain has been mismanaged with great skill
> All he believes are his eyes
> And his eyes they just tell lies ("License to Kill")

> All the truth in the world adds up to one big lie ("Things
>   Have Changed")

---

[5] Augustine, *On Free Choice of the Will* (Indianapolis: Bobbs-Merrill, 1964), p. 128.

The second penalty, difficulty, also has universal manifestations. We are all vexed by pain in this world. Again, in Dylan's words:

> There's a whole lot of people suffering tonight
> From the disease of conceit
> Whole lot of people struggling tonight
> From the disease of conceit ("Disease of Conceit")

Indeed, the phrase "disease of conceit" is a good terse summation of the Augustinian doctrine of original sin, capturing as it does some key features of the concept. Like many diseases, our moral corruption is contagious (via natural reproduction) and has ruinous effects. It is fatal, in fact, as death itself is a result of the fall. Original sin is also, at its core, a kind of conceit, a profound vanity and self-importance of which our token sins are mere symptoms. Numerous vices can be reduced to the basic impulse to place oneself before others. It's no wonder that Jesus Christ formulated the Golden Rule as he did. Doing to others as you would be done by counteracts selfishness and so cuts off many vices at the root.

Death Is Not the End

Such a pessimistic view of human nature prompts one to ask, "What good am I?" Or, more generally, what remains of human dignity?

> Wise man lookin' in a blade of grass
> Young man lookin' in the shadows that pass
> Poor man lookin' through painted glass
> For dignity
> Searchin' high, searchin' low
> Searchin' everywhere I know
> Askin' the cops wherever I go
> Have you seen dignity? ("Dignity")

The Augustinian reply is that human dignity resides in the divine spark within every one of us. Though marred by sin and in need of redemption, each of us has an immortal soul whose worth is immeasurable. This idea is not an entirely Christian invention, of course, but dates to the earliest days of Western philosophy. According to Socrates, "The soul is most like that which is divine, immortal, intelligible, uniform, indissoluble, and ever self-consistent and invariable."[6]

Thus, as Dylan says, "death is not the end." His hope for life beyond the grave in "the land of permanent bliss" emerges frequently in his songs. Sometimes Dylan expresses confidence about his own fate:

> And I'm still carrying that gift you gave
> It's a part of me now, it's been cherished and saved
> It'll be with me unto the grave
> And then unto eternity ("In the Summertime")

Other times he is less sure:

> I've been walking that lonesome valley
> Trying to get to heaven before they close the door ("Tryin' to
>   Get to Heaven")

But one thing does seem certain for Dylan, and that is that more life awaits us in eternity: "Though you might call it 'Paradise'" ("The Ballad of Frankie Lee and Judas Priest"). In his liner notes to the *Biograph* album, Dylan declares, "I think that this world is just a passing-through place and that the dead have eyes."[7]

And after his brush with death because of a heart infection in 1997, he remarked, "I really thought I'd be seeing Elvis soon."[8]

Socrates taught that wisdom is the way to God. And a philosopher is someone devoted to gaining wisdom. In fact the term "philosopher" literally means "lover of wisdom." Most people live as slaves to their physical desires, preoccupied with how they look, what they own, and how they can fill their stomachs. When these are a person's chief pursuits, the soul is essentially a prisoner of the body. The only way of escape is to deny

---

[6] Plato, *The Collected Dialogues of Plato* (Princeton: Princeton University Press, 1961), *Phaedo*, 80b.

[7] Scott Marshall and Marcia Ford, *Restless Pilgrim: The Spiritual Journey of Bob Dylan* (Lake Mary: Relevant Books, 2002), p. 83.

[8] *Restless Pilgrim*, p. 125.

the body's urges and purify the soul, which, according to Socrates, is the essence of wisdom. Every soul will face a destiny in the afterlife befitting its earthly conduct. The wise, says Socrates, will find rest with God, while "the wicked . . . are compelled to wander about [Hades] as a punishment for their bad conduct in the past."[9]

This theme is echoed by Dylan:

> Am I ready? Hope I'm ready
> When destruction cometh swiftly and there's no time to say
>   fare-thee-well
> Have you decided whether you want to be
> In heaven or in hell?
> Are you ready for the judgment?
> Are you ready for that terrible swift sword? ("Are You
>   Ready?")

This is scary stuff. It's enough to make a person a bit anxious about dying. If there is a divine judgment, then how do you know you are ready to stand the test? Socrates answers as follows:

> There is one way, then, in which a man can be free from all anxiety about the fate of his soul—if in life he has abandoned bodily pleasures and adornments, as foreign to his purpose and likely to do more harm than good, and has devoted himself to the pleasures of acquiring knowledge, and so by decking his soul not with a borrowed beauty but with his own—with self-control, and goodness, and courage, and liberality, and truth—has fitted himself to await his journey to the next world.[10]

Okay, so it has to do with virtue, living a good, solid moral life. Augustine would certainly agree, to a point. Moral goodness, he would say, is *necessary* but not *sufficient* by itself for salvation. Divine mercy is also vital. After all, something must overcome the terrible reign of original sin in the human heart. That something, of course, is grace—unmerited divine favor. So, confesses Dylan:

---

[9] Plato, *Phaedo*, 81d.
[10] Plato, *Phaedo*, 114d–115a.

If You find it in Your heart, can I be forgiven?
Guess I owe You some kind of apology
I've escaped death so many times, I know I'm only living
By the saving grace that's over me
Well, the death of life, then come the resurrection
Wherever I am welcome is where I'll be
I put all my confidence in Him, my sole protection
Is the saving grace that's over me ("Saving Grace")

As for the moral goodness that we are able to achieve, this is itself ultimately a divine gift. Speaking to God, Augustine puts it this way: "The good I do is done by you in me and by your grace."[11]

Similarly, Socrates says, "Whoever has virtue gets it by divine dispensation."[12]

Look Up, Look Up

Immanuel Kant maintained that three philosophical postulates are necessary to account for human moral responsibility: God, freedom, and immortality. Without freedom, no moral praise or blame for conduct is possible. Without God, there is no worthy moral judge for our conduct, nor is there a sufficiently powerful force to dole out rewards and punishments. And unless humans are immortal, there is no way for us to experience those consequences of our actions. These Kantian intuitions are well illustrated in Dylan's lyrics, as we have seen. The master songsmith provides yet another confirmation that this triad of postulates is at least coherent. The question of their truth, of course, is another matter. Some, such as Kierkegaard, have preferred to see religious convictions like God's existence and human immortality as matters for faith only. Others, such as Aquinas and Descartes, have attempted to rationally demonstrate their truth. But even their confidence had its limits, recognizing that religious conviction must allow for mystery, and faith must trust where reason cannot venture. Indeed, as Dylan says, "Some things are too hot to touch / The human mind can only stand so much" ("Things Have Changed").

---

[11] Augustine, *Confessions* (New York: Penguin, 1961), p. 209.
[12] Plato, *Meno*, 100b.

13

Busy Being Born Again: Bob Dylan's Christian Philosophy

FRANCIS J. BECKWITH

> Mary wore three links of chain
> Every link was Jesus name
> Keep your hand on that plow, hold on
> Oh Lord, Oh Lord, keep your hand on that plow, hold on
> (Bob Dylan, *Gospel Plow*)

These lyrics are from "Gospel Plow," a traditional folk song that Bob Dylan sang on his first album, *Bob Dylan*. Although released in 1962, this song would be, by most accounts of Dylan's life and work, better suited for his so-called "Christian albums," issued between 1979 and 1981. But I think there is reason to reject that judgment, and to view these latter albums— *Slow Train Coming*, *Saved*, and *Shot of Love*—and the theological instruction Dylan offers his listeners in them, not as isolated from his larger body of work, but part of a lifelong project to come to grips with the deeper moral and metaphysical questions that have always found a place in Dylan's art, both before and after his Christian conversion.

Strengthen the Things that Remain

Bob Dylan's conversion to Christianity was, to say the least, controversial for several reasons.[1] Dylan was born into a Jewish

---

[1] See Howard Sounes, *Down the Highway: The Life of Bob Dylan* (New York: Grove Press, 2001), pp. 306–351.

family, and as is well known, conversions from Judaism to Christianity are extremely rare. Dylan's conversion to *evangelical* Christianity, known for its political conservatism and its view of the Bible as an inerrant guide to history, theological truth, and ethics, was particularly shocking because of Dylan's place in the cultural revolution of the 1960s. With the exception of the civil rights movement[2] and to a lesser extent the anti-war movement, the components of the sixties revolution can trace their philosophical roots and activist inspiration to the writings of non-religious, secular intellectuals.

Yet, if one carefully inspects Dylan's Christian albums, one will find an individual who found in the Christian faith an account of the deep moral and social principles that had been lurking behind his pre-Christian work for quite some time. I believe there are four aspects of Dylan's pre-Christian work that support this conclusion.

Dylan's Assimilation of the Christian Narrative

In his autobiography, *Chronicles: Volume One*, Dylan tells his readers about his own intellectual development and the books and writers he had read in the early stages of his career in Greenwich Village.[3] These books, though not treatises on theology, and their writers, not always Christians or sympathetic to the cause of Christ, are works and thinkers that were immersed in, shaped by, reacting to, or influenced the formation of the Christian narrative.

What is the Christian narrative? It is, in its broadest terms, a story of betrayal, separation, and redemption that has a beginning, a middle, and an end. It is a linear history that began at some finite point in the past and is destined to end at some point in the future, the eschaton. Specifically, the Christian narrative is the story of humanity's relationship to God, humanity's separation from God, the reconciliation of one with the other by means of the death and resurrection of God's Son, and His eventual return and the establishment of his Kingdom on earth.

---

[2] See Charles Marsh, *The Beloved Community: How Faith Shapes Social Justice, from the Civil Rights Movement to Today* (New York: Basic Books, 2005).
[3] Bob Dylan, *Chronicles: Volume One* (New York: Simon and Schuster, 2004), pp. 36–39.

Dylan's fascination with and interest in the American Civil War and the years surrounding it, which he conveys in his autobiography, is illustrative of his assimilation of the Christian narrative.[4] Comparing America of the early 1960s with America between 1855 and 1865, Dylan writes:

> The age that I was living in didn't resemble that age, but yet it did in some mysterious and traditional way. Not just a little bit, but a lot. There was a broad spectrum and commonwealth that I was living upon, and the basic psychology of that life was every bit a part of it. If you turned the light towards it, you could see the full complexity of human nature. *Back there, America was put on the cross, died, and was resurrected.* There was nothing synthetic about it. *The godawful truth of that would be the all-encompassing template behind everything that I would write.*[5]

Dylan's prolific employment of the Hebrew-Christian Scriptures in his pre-Christian work is well-known and well-documented.[6] But what is not often appreciated is that Dylan's use of these sacred writings is the result of how deeply the Christian narrative is embedded in his worldview, as the above quote indicates, for these writings have within them stories, characters, moral lessons, and principles that convey truths about human nature, society, justice, loss, and redemption that resonate with Dylan's intuitions. His use of Scripture clearly was not gratuitous.

Unlike other artists who came of age in the 1960s and 1970s but have not really grown up, Dylan has matured as both an artist and a thinker, but with his philosophical worldview firmly intact. For example, if his first two Christian albums—*Slow Train* and *Saved*—are Dylan's affirmation of New Testament faith and hope, then his Book of Ecclesiastes is *Time Out of Mind*, an album for which Dylan won the 1998 Grammy Award for album of the year. It is the reflections of a man who still trusts in God ("I know God is my shield, and he won't lead me astray" ["'Til I Fell in Love with You"]), but at the same time longs for lost love and fleeting youth ("All the young men with the young women lookin' so good / Well, I'd trade places with any of them

---

[4] Dylan, pp. 84–86.
[5] Dylan, p. 86 (emphasis added).
[6] See Michael J. Gilmour, *Tangled Up in the Bible: Bob Dylan and Scripture* (New York: Continuum, 2004).

/ In a minute, if I could" ["Highlands"]). The man who asked us to "[j]ust remember that death is not the end" ("Death Is Not the End"), now tells of his reluctance to leave this mortal realm ("I was born here and I'll die here against my will" ["Not Dark Yet"]) as well as the difficulty of remaining ("Sometimes my burden seems more than I can bear / It's not dark yet, but it's getting there" ["Not Dark Yet"]). _Time_ concludes with the twelve minute "Highlands," a foreboding folk-rock ballad of disconnected reflections of an aging rock star at the height of his creative powers, daring to answer the question he asked a jilted lover in 1965, "How does it feel?" ("Like a Rolling Stone"). The answer then was: "When you ain't got nothing, you got nothing to lose." The answer now, from the song "Tryin' To Get to Heaven," is: "When you think you've lost everything / You find out you can always lose a little more."

In 2003, Dylan accepted an invitation from Mel Gibson to view his movie _The Passion of the Christ_ prior to its release in the hopes that Dylan would write an original song for the soundtrack.[7] Because of time constraints, Dylan was not able to view the movie until after it was released in February 2004. Nevertheless, Dylan did offer to cover the hymn "Rock of Ages" for the CD _Passion of The Christ: Songs_ (Lost Keyword, 2004). But the record label rejected Dylan's offer. So, he suggested the song "Not Dark Yet," a piece that appeared on _Time Out of Mind_. It appeared on a 2004 CD, _The Passion of the Christ: Songs Inspired By_ (Universal South, 2004).

We Live in a Moral Universe.

Dylan's lyrics—especially those with which he issues moral judgments or makes moral claims—presuppose that we live in a moral universe, one in which moral law is part of the infra-structure of reality. According to this view, which philosophers sometimes call "moral realism," the universe is not simply a complex collection of material parts, but one that is the home

---

[7] I learned this in personal conversation and correspondence with popular music writer and president of MJM Entertainment Group, Mark Joseph, who is author of the book, _Faith, God, and Rock + Roll: From Bono to Jars of Clay: How People of Faith Are Transforming American Popular Music_ (Grand Rapids: Baker Book House, 2003).

of creatures who have immaterial moral properties that are acquired and developed by the exercise of virtue in obedience to the directives of a moral law. What does this mean? To employ an illustration, when we cite Mother Teresa as an exemplar of virtue, we are saying that she possesses certain moral properties that we detect in her actions, such as patience, kindness, mercy, love, and good judgment, and from which we draw the conclusion "Mother Teresa is good." Goodness is neither a material property, like height or weight, nor an empirical description, like hair color or tone of voice. It is an immaterial property that we can "see" in certain people as a result of the example of personal virtue they set for us. Because human beings have an intrinsic moral purpose that may be directed by the will of each agent, one's virtue, one's moral excellence, is dependent upon the choices one makes because those choices shape the direction and quality of one's character.

Dylan's pre-Christian work embodies this understanding. In "The Lonesome Death of Hattie Carroll," Dylan scolds those "who philosophize disgrace and criticize all fears." He seems to be passing judgment on those who are incapable of seeing clear cases of virtue and vice because they have incorporated into their moral sense an interpretative grid of complex rationalizations that suppress the knowledge of this moral reality, exemplified by their philosophizing of disgrace and criticizing of all fears. It's as if Dylan had in mind the same understanding St. Paul had when he issued this judgment in his letter to the Romans: "The wrath of God is being revealed from heaven against all the godlessness and wickedness of men who suppress the truth by their wickedness, since what may be known about God is plain to them, because God has made it plain to them" (Romans 1:18–19, NIV).

In one of his post-conversion compositions not connected to his 1979–81 Christian period, "Dignity" (released on *Greatest Hits Vol. III*) Dylan sings, "Someone showed me a picture and I just laughed / Dignity never been photographed." This means that "dignity," unlike a physical or an empirical entity, cannot be measured or observed by our instruments or sense organs. This seems to indicate that Dylan thinks of "dignity" as a real irreducible moral property, something that connects well with a Christian worldview, one in which immaterial properties and beings (goodness, virtue, God, souls) are plentiful.[8] Dignity cannot take up space, be heard, be seen, or make you fat if you ingest too much of it. And yet, we are more certain and more sure of our dignity and its properties than we are of whether quarks exist or whether Pluto is a lifeless world at the far end of the solar system. You can't "find" dignity, Dylan deftly explains, if you're looking for it with the wrong senses: "Somebody got murdered on New Year's Eve / Somebody said dignity was the first to leave."

The Moral Law Is Objectively True

Given the fact that we live in a moral universe, there exist fundamental principles of justice and morality that are unchanging and forever true. This is in contrast to moral relativism, the view that moral principles are relative to either the individual or his or her culture.[9]

Take, for example, "With God on Our Side," a song in which Dylan presents the history of modern warfare and conflict between peoples (from the Old American West through the Cold War era) and shows that appeal to God's favor on the part of one side has been employed to justify all sorts of atrocities against human beings. He even raises the question of why Judas Iscariot could not offer the same sort of argument to justify his betrayal of Jesus of Nazareth:

> Through many a dark hour
> I've been thinkin' about this
> That Jesus Christ
> Was betrayed by a kiss
> But I can't think for you
> You'll have to decide
> Whether Judas Iscariot
> Had God on his side

---

[8] See Francis J. Beckwith, William Lane Craig, and J.P. Moreland, eds., *To Everyone an Answer: A Case for the Christian Worldview* (Downers Grove: InterVarsity Press, 2004).

[9] For a popular presentation and critique of moral relativism, see Francis J. Beckwith and Gregory P. Koukl, *Relativism: Feet Firmly Planted in Mid-Air* (Grand Rapids: Baker Book House, 1998).

It would be a mistake to understand this song as a general indictment against American Christianity. Rather, it is an indictment against religious people, especially Christians, who have drifted from the absolute moral principles that they claim to accept. This is why the ironic question about Judas in this stanza is so biting. Only if his audience, and Dylan himself, had embraced the Christian narrative and its moral foundation would this song and this stanza have the meaning and impact that they do. In his first Christian album, *Slow Train Coming*, Dylan employs the same type of ironic reasoning to issue judgments similar to those made in "With God on Our Side":

> Adulterers in churches and pornography in the schools
> You got gangsters in power and lawbreakers making rules
> . . .
> Spiritual advisors and gurus to guide your every move
> Instant inner peace and every step you take has got to be
>   approved ("When You Gonna Wake Up?")

> Big-time negotiators, false healers and woman haters
> Masters of the bluff and masters of the proposition
> But the enemy I see
> Wears a cloak of decency
> All non-believers and men stealers talkin' in the name of
>   religion
> . . .
> People starving and thirsting, grain elevators are bursting
> Oh, you know it costs more to store the food than it do to
>   give it
> They say lose your inhibitions
> Follow your own ambitions
> They talk about a life of brotherly love show me someone
>   who knows
> how to live it (*Slow Train*)

If morality were merely relative to time, place, or individual, it's not clear on what grounds Dylan could make these judgments about past injustices and theological illegitimacy. Only if Dylan believes that there is an unchanging standard of right and wrong can one make sense of Dylan's moral judgments in both his pre- and post-conversion songs and why these pieces, though separated by many years and circumstances, appear to be seamlessly connected to a similar, if not the same, moral tradition.

Even in "The Times They Are A-Changin'" it's the *times*, not the moral principles, that are changing. We know this because Dylan appeals to an ancient understanding of the last judgment found in the Christian Bible: "And the first one now will later be last."[10] Apparently, for Dylan, the times were changing because there was a hearkening back to first principles that should have been but were not applied to those who were oppressed and for whose cause in the American civil rights movement Dylan offered support. Not coincidentally, these are the same sort of principles that animated Abraham Lincoln, the American president who dominated the era that fascinated Dylan as a young folksinger:

> Four score and seven years ago our fathers brought forth on this continent, a new nation, conceived in Liberty, and dedicated to the proposition that all men are created equal . . . It is rather for us to be here dedicated to the great task remaining before us—that from these honored dead we take increased devotion to that cause for which they gave the last full measure of devotion—that we here highly resolve that these dead shall not have died in vain—that this nation, under God, shall have a new birth of freedom—and that government of the people, by the people, for the people, shall not perish from the earth.[11]

For Lincoln, the "new birth of freedom" was the consummation of the promise of liberty and equality found in the principles of the American founding. The times, for Lincoln, were a-changin' because the times were finally catching up to the moral truths, promised at the nation's genesis though eternal in their patrimony. In "Blowin' in the Wind" injustices that stretch across space and time are picked out, and a question is asked as to when they will end:

---

[10] Jesus said, "But many that are first shall be last; and the last shall be first" (Matthew 19:30, KJV).

[11] Abraham Lincoln, "Gettysburg Address" (19th November, 1863), http://showcase.netins.net/web/creative/lincoln/speeches/gettysburg.htm (accessed December 2nd, 2004).

How many years can a mountain exist
Before it's washed to the sea?
Yes, 'n' how many years can some people exist
Before they're allowed to be free?
Yes, 'n' how many times can a man turn his head
Pretending he just doesn't see?
. . .
How many times must a man look up
Before he can see the sky?
Yes, 'n' how many ears must one man have
Before he can hear people cry?
Yes, 'n' how many deaths will it take till he knows
That too many people have died?

The moral judgments that Dylan issues in his songs span cultures and eras and thus do not make any sense unless Dylan believes there is an objective moral law, one that is universal, unchanging, and applies to all persons in all times and in all places. Perhaps this is why in his 2001 song "High Water (for Charlie Patton)" Dylan offers this assessment of the "open-mindedness" associated with naive relativism:

Well, George Lewis told the Englishman, the Italian and the
     Jew
"You can't open your mind, boys
To every conceivable point of view"

It Is Important that We Practice Virtue

According to Dylan, one should live justly for its own sake. He writes in "Forever Young," a song that reads like a prayer to a young person, perhaps one of Dylan's own children:

May God bless and keep you always
May your wishes all come true
May you always do for others
And let others do for you
. . .
May you grow up to be righteous
May you grow up to be true
May you always know the truth

And see the lights surrounding you
May you always be courageous
Stand upright and be strong

In the "The Lonesome Death of Hattie Carroll," Dylan describes the negligent homicide of a kitchen maid, Hattie Carroll, at the hands of the son of a Baltimore aristocrat, William Zanzinger, who killed Ms. Carroll "[w]ith a cane that he twirled around his diamond ring finger / At a Baltimore hotel society gath'rin'." Dylan insists that the aristocrat's penalty—six months in jail—does not fit the crime:

In the courtroom of honor, the judge pounded his gavel
To show that all's equal and that the courts are on the level
And that the strings in the books ain't pulled and persuaded
And that even the nobles get properly handled
Once that the cops have chased after and caught 'em
And that the ladder of law has no top and no bottom
Stared at the person who killed for no reason
Who just happened to be feelin' that way without warnin'
And he spoke through his cloak, most deep and distin-
    guished
And handed out strongly, for penalty and repentance
William Zanzinger with a six-month sentence

There's no utilitarian calculus here. The penalty, according to Dylan, was wrong regardless of the "consequences." What concerned Dylan was not whether the victim's family received a just remedy for its loss, but whether just retribution was provided to the assailant. The Biblical *lex talionis,* the law of retribution,[12] was what Dylan seemed to have in mind.

In "What Good Am I?" a song that appeared on the album *Oh Mercy,* Dylan offers some personal reflections on the importance of virtue, almost reversing the questions asked in "Blowin' in the Wind" and turning them on himself:

---

[12] "The law of retaliation an example of which is given in the law of Moses, an eye for an eye, a tooth for a tooth, etc." ("Lex Talionis," in *Legal Law Terms,* http://www.legallawterms.com/Legal.asp-Definition-LEX%20TALIONIS [accessed December 30th, 2004]).

What good am I if I'm like all the rest
If I just turn away, when I see how you're dressed
If I shut myself off so I can't hear you cry
What good am I?
What good am I if I know and don't do
If I see and don't say, if I look right through you
If I turn a deaf ear to the thunderin' sky
What good am I?

One hears in these philosophical reflections echoes from the Book of James: "What does it profit, my brethren, if a man says he has faith but has not works? Can his faith save him? If a brother or sister is ill-clad and in lack of daily food, and one of you says to them, 'Go in peace, be warmed and filled,' without giving them the things needed for the body, what does it profit? So faith by itself, if it has no works, is dead" (James 2:14–17, RSV).

A Call to Unchanging Truths

Bob Dylan's conversion to Christianity is consistent with the deeper metaphysical and moral commitments that have always percolated beneath the surface of his art. Unlike the nihilism and historicism that one finds in other artists both in rock and folk, Dylan's call to moral or spiritual reformation is a call back to those unchanging truths—those first principles—that we have forgotten, either out of negligence, human weakness, or a willful disdain for the good, the true, and the beautiful. But alas, everything must end, and repentance and redemption is possible, if you look in the right place: "Just as sure as we're living, just as sure as you're born / Look up, look up—seek your Maker—'fore Gabriel blows his horn" (Sugar Baby).[13]

---

[13] This essay is dedicated to my colleague, Marc H. Ellis, University Professor of American and Jewish Studies, and Director of the Center for American and Jewish Studies, Baylor University. Although we are separated by politics and faith, we are united by Baylor and Dylan.

14

Language on the Lam(b): Tarantula in Dylan and Nietzsche

DAVID GOLDBLATT and
EDWARD NECARSULMER IV

Some of Bob Dylan's best work is sweet and plain, simple and direct. While adept at the deep language of pain, personal and political, Dylan is rarely self-pitying or indulgent. Staying above the fray, his deadpan voice is a paradigm of indifference to the subject matter of his lyrics, cross-grained to their content and melody. Then there are his songs that are open to wide interpretation, as if they were everybody's autobiography. For yet others, powerful though they may be, something is happening here but you don't know what it is. However, with the possible exception of some early liner notes, nothing Dylan has done thus far comes as close to a radical departure from an ordinary read than his book *Tarantula*. *Tarantula* contains ribbons of language that are at once extraordinarily imaginative while at first and further glances incapable of explanation.

It is Dylan's best show at being very, very funny.

One hundred and twenty-five years or so before *Spider-Man* (the movie), the great German philosopher Friedrich Nietzsche (1844–1900) wrote "The Tarantulas" as one of the more important sections of his most widely read book, *Thus Spoke Zarathustra: A Book for No One and for Everyone* (the full title). In this chapter we'd like to explain what makes *Tarantula* work when it does and to compare it with certain aspects of Nietzsche's book, especially and obviously "The Tarantulas." [1]

---

[1] Friedrich Nietzsche, *Thus Spoke Zarathustra* (New York: Viking, 1966), pp. 99–102.

Ordinarily, this would involve something like an aesthetic theory—a theory about artworks, audiences, artists, and creative processes. However, the intuitive artist evades theory in a certain way, and so we will try to offer an account of what makes a spontaneous Bob Dylan successful despite the "difficult" read it may still present to his curious, ardent, hopeful readers. To do this we will turn some attention to a certain healthy perversion of metaphor called "catachresis," which we explain later on.

Two Tarantulas

Being the philologist he was, Nietzsche makes explicit the etymological relationship between the spider and the whirling music and dance tarantella, rooted in the Italian town of Tarantos, where the bite of the spider was said to cause the illness tarantism, a malady typified by an uncontrollable urge to dance wildly, which supposedly reached epidemic proportions in sixteenth-century Europe. Dylan was twenty-three years old when he started work on *Tarantula*. He was already too accomplished to deny his sort of genius and too famous to walk the streets in daylight. As the book was about to go to press, his legendary Woodstock motorcycle accident (1966) put things on hold. It was published in 1971, long years of absence later. The cover of our edition says "novel" but it is hardly that. It was published again in 1994 as *Tarantula Poems,* but calling everything in it poetry or even prose poetry would be something of a stretch.

Years later Dylan said, "There was no difficulty in writing it at all, it just wasn't a book, it was a nuisance. It didn't have that certain quality which now I think a book should have. It didn't have any structure at all, it was just one flow. It flowed for ninety pages . . . they were short little lines, nothing within a big framework. I couldn't even conceive of doing anything in a big framework at that time."[2] Dylan said it himself: *Tarantula* lacks narrative structure, even if one or two of the "characters" like aretha pop up now and then. However, *Tarantula* exhibits several overall consistencies. For example, the book is divided

---

[2] From an interview in Craig McGregor, ed., *Bob Dylan, The Early Years: A Retrospective*, (Cambridge, Massachsetts: Da Capo, 1990), p. 289. This interview was published originally in *Sing Out*, October–November 1968.

throughout into short, titled sections beginning with something like a description of a circumstance, a slice of life of some person, someone usually named early on and encountered by and involved with the narrator, who we could call "Dylan." Most every section closes with a letter or short memo, ending with a different closing salutation. The signatory name of each letter is different from every other, but the content and style is consistent enough to recognize the same author throughout (same *author function* to use Michel Foucault's term). It is as if these multiple signings exemplified the artist's license for the relocation of biography. What Dylan is right about is his use of the word "flow" as in "stream of consciousness." Words and expressions that *seem* to come to Dylan intuitively and unfiltered. In fact, *Tarantula* is very much a series of unrestrained *non sequiturs* and self-interruptions, and the segments are required to work together only as little as a collection of poetry by a single writer. Nevertheless, those expecting Dylan's brilliance here and there would not be disappointed. It is original and curious. There's no question that the style of the writing, consistent throughout, and Dylan's smart-assed, edgy attitude are its most prominent features. Wit dominates, but there is also wisdom.

In *Ecce Homo*, where Nietzsche explains the origins of his ideas for *Zarathustra*, he compares understanding it to understanding music. "The whole of *Zarathustra* might perhaps be reckoned as music—certainly a rebirth of the art of *hearing* was a precondition of it,"[3] he says. Not unexpectedly, Dylan's *Tarantula*, too, is best read aloud and is woven through with mentions of song and dance. It would do well to offer a sample from its opening lines—one not entirely atypical for much of Dylan's book.

Guns, the Falcon's Mouthbook & Gashcat Unpunished
aretha/ crystal jukebox queen of hymn & him diffused in
drunk transfusion wound would heed sweet soundwave
crippled & cry salute to oh great particular el dorado reel
& ye battered personal god but she cannot she the leader of
whom when ye follow, she cannot she has no back she

---

[3] Friedrich Nietzsche, *Ecce Homo* (London: Penguin, 1979), p. 69.

cannot. . .beneath black flowery railroad fans & fig leaf
shades & dogs of all nite joes, grow like arches & cures the
harmonica battalions of bitter cowards, bones & bygones
while what steadier louder the moans & arms of funeral
landlord with one passionate kiss rehearse from dusk &
climbing into the bushes with some favorite enemy ripping
the postage stamps & crazy mailmen & waving all rank &
familiar ambition than that itself, is needed to know that
mother is not a lady[4]

Part of our work in this chapter will be to locate certain
aspects of *Tarantula* we feel are relevant aesthetic features,
aspects important for its interpretation and appreciation and that
is what we begin to do next.

The Giving of Advice, the Renaming of Names

Dylan's artworld is heavily populated, but *Tarantula,* the occa-
sion for small visits with wall-to-wall people, is packed. Mostly,
we find the narrator with street-side seats to many intimate lives,
encountering them, knowing them, and somehow being
involved. We see this involvement with creatures of various
sorts, animate and inanimate, in *Zarathustra.* Nietzsche calls
what Zarathustra is doing "teachings" as in "I teach you the
Overman" (the famous *Übermensch* or beyond man), advocat-
ing a set of character traits or virtues of a possible future being,
not Zarathustra himself and not Nietzsche. Its best example may
be the artist. Generally, the Overman is a universal character, a
value still open to interpretation, but a standard by which the
present walkers of the earth can measure their own shortcomings in the absence of the standard of a God, whose power is
sinking like the sun on the face of Europe, Nietzsche says.

Similarly, what Dylan often does is give *advice* (a banal
word, yes). His 1964 lengthy "Advice for Geraldine on Her
Miscellaneous Birthday" closes with "when asked / t'give your
real name . . . never give it."[5] Some chapter titles in *Tarantula*

---

[4] Bob Dylan, *Tarantula* (New York: Macmillan, 1971), p. 1. Hereafter cited parenthetically in text.
[5] Bob Dylan, "Advice for Geraldine on Her Miscellaneous Birthday," in
Writings and Drawings (New York: Knopf, 1973), pp. 118–19.

are called "Advice to . . . " Dylan's advice is often advice as in "I'd advise you to leave town." But this points out a difference between Dylan in *Tarantula* and Nietzsche's *Zarathustra*, or if you will, the difference between the advice of art and the teachings of philosophy. In philosophy, it seems the teachings are as abstract and general or universal as can be justified by some criterion or other. Dylan's advice is personal and particular, anchored in the quotidian circumstances of individuals and not really intended, we think, to go beyond them—unless, of course, the shoe fits, as it often does.

The letters in *Tarantula* are especially advice-laden. For example, he says, "why don't you learn to / dance instead of looking for new / friends?" or "dear tom / have i ever told you that I / think your name ought to be / bill" or "how come youre / so afraid to stop talking?" or "perhaps you ought to change your line of / work. you know. like how long can someone / of your caliber continue to paint pencil / sharpeners." Or "forget about those / hollywood people telling you what to do— / theyre all gonna get killed by the Indians— / see you in your dreams." And "just / remember tho, when you evaluate a piece of / butter, you are talking abut yourself, so / you'd just better sign your name" and "give up—give up—the ship is lost: go / back to san bernardino—stop trying to / organize the crew—it's every man for / himself—are you a man or a self?" And, "your problem is that you / wanna better word for world" (pp. 31, 37, 40, 58–59, 91, 94, 81, 24 respectivly). It's advice that seems to be neither tactful nor altruistic. No one gives Dylan advice.

Zarathustra, in going down from his mountain retreat, comes upon creatures of wide variety. He preaches to tightrope walkers, dwarfs, snakes, eagles, dancing girls, a motley cow, and, of course, a tarantula, among others, and is first seen speaking to the sun. Dylan's book is a looking-down-upon, and his book is characterized most blatantly by the swirl of names sweeping *Tarantula* into a consistency: they could be opposites of the names of debutantes, the non-preppy nicknames of the unbourgeois, those, as he puts it, from "the greyhound circuit," where he surely finds a certain source of inspiration, something, we imagine, quite different, richer, more fun, and, in a sense, more real and accurate, from the birth names of Hibbing. Nicknames are, or should be, ripe for philosophical analysis, lying somewhere between proper names that refer or designate only and definite descriptions where *sense* as well as reference generate meaning. Being between in this way, they name individuals and bring to mind archetypes, and Dylan seems to like this dual aspect of renaming. In *Tarantula*, names are occasions for humor or mockery, certainly part of the language of the street.

Nicknames, of course, are not pseudonyms—the latter being emblems of anonymity, a valued property the famous leave at the door, the former signs of some type of intimacy. We might recall that in the 1974 movie *Pat Garrett and Billy the Kid*, Dylan, not his own name until later in life, plays a drifter named "Alias." We can't say where Dylan got these names, if he picked up names like these from real people he encountered in his early New York days, or if he is naming fictions as did Scottie (the invalided Jimmy Stewart character) in Alfred Hitchcock's 1954 classic *Rear Window*, naming Miss Lonelyhearts, Miss Torso, Songwriter and the like from what he sees voyeuristically at a distance across his downtown courtyard. In *Chronicles: Volume One*, we find Bob Dylan comparing the gangsters Al Capone and Pretty Boy Floyd. Dylan says that Capone is "not even worthy enough to have a name," meaning a nickname. Then he says, "Pretty Boy Floyd, on the other hand, stirs up an adventurous spirit . . . his name has something to say . . . He'll never rule over a city, can't manipulate the machine or bend people to his will, yet he's the stuff of real flesh and blood, represents humanity in general and gives you an impression of power. At least before they trapped him in the boonies."[6] Dylan's vision of humanity is intimately tied to those who are "real flesh and blood," and Dylan's art has taken its turn towards those culturally bound to acquire new names in lieu of their own. It is this portion of humanity that had lured Dylan, first into folk songs and then into the revolutionary lyrics of his rock music. But, as we shall see, the idea of street names replacing birth names and the cultural intimacy that lowly baptism tends to promote and embody is central to Dylan's only book-length effort besides *Chronicles*.

In *Tarantula* we find names like Sir Cringe, Froggy, Franky Duck, Zorba the Bomb, Zeke the Cork, Shorty Cookie, Pig, Willy

---

[6] Bob Dylan, *Chronicles: Volume One* (New York: Simon and Schuster, 2004). p. 39.

Purple, to name the signers of the letters, and Peewee the Ear, Jake the Flesh, prince goulash, Micky McMicky, Jack of Spades, Mrs. Actually, Phombus Pucker, crow jane, and "a strange man we're calling Simply That" (p. 26), to list some of the hundred other names. And then there's his line, "I'm just a scientist. i / ain't got no name" (p. 8). Those named are not couch potatoes or mowers of lawns, and Dylan finds literature in their explosion of life. There is art in these names—the names people call themselves or the names others call them, and they are more akin to titles than are Tom, Dick, and Harry—names hooked to gendered entities while still blankish slates. "I have a problem sometimes remembering someone's real name," Dylan explains in *Chronicles*, "so I give them another one, something that more accurately describes them."[7]

The names he uses and the everyday jobs had by those named are indicators of the kind of people he engages, and in Dylan's spun or constructed neighborhood they form the web holding *Tarantula* together. In addition, the book is riddled with names of the famous and not so famous, mostly politicos and show-biz folks, especially musicians of virtually every type. But while the famous get mentioned, it is the ordinary folks who are addressed. Those named are mostly proletarian and *lumpenproletarian,* and Dylan mentions their occupations, jobs such as ambulance driver, window washer, garbage man, truck driver, gambler, scrubwoman, newsboy, stripper, car thief, and petty gangster. Dylan often talks down to those he addresses with a tone that is sometimes admonishing, usually articulating faults, troubles and flaws, dislikes and petty irritations.

Resentment and Revenge

In "The Tarantulas" Zarathustra tells the "secretly vengeful" spider, "Your poison makes the soul whirl with revenge." And, in homage to Odysseus, he says, "To keep me from whirling my friends, tie me tight to this column. Rather would I be a stylite [a Christian ascetic of old] even, than a whirl of revenge."[8] It is Zarathustra's way to the highest hope "that man be delivered

---

[7] Dylan, *Chronicles*, p. 169
[8] Nietzsche, *Zarathustra*, p. 102.

from revenge." Nietzsche understands *ressentiment*, that think-ing-against, the poisoning of the soul at the heart of slave morality. Not only directed at others, the decadent forces of *ressentiment* are gathered against the "it was" and are anti-thetical to Nietzsche's general advice of *amor fati*, loving what-ever it is that is one's fate—the past we can no longer change: "The will cannot will backwards." [9] Moreover, and contrary to a popular misconception of him, Nietzsche recognizes a bridge to the political and the social where honorific terms like equal-ity and justice are utilized as masks for what is really revenge, most obviously in the realms of punishment, persecution, and war. For Nietzsche, with the possible exception of Socratic rea-son, nothing kills a will to art more than the rear view gaze of compulsive blame and self-pity, and we can think here of Dylan's line, "She's an artist, she don't look back" ("She Belongs to Me").

In "Idiot Wind," for example, Dylan explores the bitterness of resentment and revenge against a lover and one's own self who botched their love. *Tarantula* has its own share of vengeful writ-ing, like when a letter says, "next time you / call me that name in a public / cafeteria, i'm just gonna haul / off & kick you so you'll feel / it. like i aint even gonna get / angry. I'm just gonna let one / fly. fix you good" (p. 48). Death and violence are scat-tered throughout *Tarantula*, like the strange section where a couple of familiar names are put to use: "here lies bob dylan / murdered / from behind / by trembling flesh / who after being refused by Lazarus / jumped on him / for solitude" (pp. 118–19). Several of the sections describe beatings like: "the bully comes in—kicks the newsboy / you know where—& begins ripping away / at the audio repairman's shirt" (p. 75). This is to say, the kind of violence Dylan espouses is akin to a kind of confusion or scattered worldview. In much the same way, there is a schism between violence in actuality (the streetfight) and violence as we most often digest it, what we see in the movies. Dylan's violence is not that of Hollywood; rather, it is decidedly primal, impulsive, and unchoreographed, necessarily embedded in language. It is the wild dance of these flailing hands and skinned knees in *Tarantula* that reveal the poison in Dylan's pen.

---

[9] Nietzsche, *Zarathustra*, p.139.

The Intuitive Artist

Christopher Ricks's excellent book, *Dylan's Visions of Sin*, contains the following comment by Dylan from Paul Zollo's *Songwriters on Songwriting*:

> As you get older, you get smarter and that can hinder you because you try to gain control over the creative impulse. Creativity is not like a freight train going down the tracks. It's something that has to be caressed and treated with a great deal of respect. If your mind is intellectually in the way, it will stop you. You've got to program your brain not to think too much.[10]

Ricks's pertinent response is: "What is at issue is not pretence but premeditation. Dylan is conscious of how much needs to be done by the unconscious or subconscious."[11] The idea of the intuitive artist, unhindered by knowing too much or knowing anything at all, is an idea as old at least as Plato's dialogue *Ion*, where Socrates refuses to credit Ion for his acclaimed performances. Socrates argues that Ion is "not in his right mind" when performing and that he is merely a medium for the voice of God. He says,

> God takes away the minds of poets, and uses them as his ministers, as he also uses diviners and holy prophets, in order that we who hear them may know them to be speaking not of themselves who utter these priceless words in a state of unconsciousness, but that God himself is the speaker, and that through them he is conversing with us.[12]

In *Ecce Homo*, where Nietzsche is recalling his inspiration for *Zarathustra*, he says something very like Plato and Dylan:

> If one had the slightest residue of superstition left in one, one would hardly be able to set aside the idea that one is merely incarnation, merely a mouthpiece, merely medium of overwhelming forces. The concept of revelation, in the sense that something sud-

---

[10] Christopher Ricks, *Dylan's Vision of Sin* (New York: HarperCollins, 2003), p. 47.

[11] Ricks, p. 47.

[12] Plato, *Ion*, in *The Dialogues of Plato*, Vol. I (New York: Random House, 1937), 534a.

denly, with unspeakable certainty and subtlety, becomes *visible*, audible . . . One hears, one does not seek; one takes, one does not ask who gives; a thought flashes up like lightning, with necessity, unfalteringly formed—I have never had a choice.[13]

Nietzsche ties his experience of being inspired by having ideas seize him with deep things he has to say about metaphor and which will lead into our Dylanesque explanation in the next section.

The involuntary nature of image, of metaphor is the most remarkable thing of all; one no longer has any idea of what is image, what metaphor, everything presents itself as the readiest, the truest, the simplest means of expression. It really does seem, to allude to a saying of Zarathustra's, as if the things themselves approached and offered themselves as metaphors . . . This is my experience of inspiration; I do not doubt that one has to go back thousands of years to find anyone who could say to me 'it is mine also.'[14]

Here, Nietzsche may have been thinking about the kind of things we'd call metaphorical when contrasting it with the literal, but for Nietzsche all language is metaphorical—it's just that some metaphors are stale and some are fresh, and this supports his idea that all thinking is interpretive or perspectival.

What we want to turn to next is a kind of language having the structure of metaphor, but metaphor where we can't quite make the connection, where we cannot slide quickly from one domain to another as with the immediacy of getting a joke. However, any prolonged encounter with Dylan's poetic intuitions is bound to run up against walls, apparent dead ends where understanding his art seems to warrant a retreat. Nevertheless, the words chosen by Dylan somehow seem to be right and contain aesthetic impacts that gain power by the very uncertainty and undecidability they create through a suspension of meaning.

The Abuse of Metaphor

Dylan's "It's Alright, Ma (I'm Only Bleeding)" contains the lines, "So don't fear if you hear / A foreign sound to your ear." A for-

---

[13] Nietzsche, *Ecce Homo*, p. 72.
[14] Nietzsche, *Ecce Homo*, p. 73.

eign sound is sometimes English put together in unfamiliar ways—we know the words, but not how they mean in this or that context, not seeing why one might follow another. What's paradoxical about Dylan's language (and this isn't terribly easy to say) is that while it includes expressions never before having seen the light of day—unused—not part of *our* "ordinary" language, they *seem* to come from some real ground, part of some down home street-talk—language Dylan might have gathered and used in his real life journeys. But we'll guess Dylan imagined them, dreamed up the names and the expressions. Consider the title from one of Dylan's most intense songs, "Idiot Wind,*"* mentioned earlier. Or, think about phrases from other of his powerful lyrics, like "warehouse eyes" from "Sad Eyed Lady of the Lowlands*"* or "reindeer armies" from "It's All Over Now Baby Blue." Or, in *Tarantula*'s opening lines, quoted previously, "harmonica battalions" and "funeral landlord." While we love Dylan for these kinds of linguistic placements, they do not shift domains easily as is the case with "sharp knife" to "sharp sports coat." The juxtaposition of expressions where the transfer initially seems blocked is called *catachresis.*

On the second page of his *Glas*, in the annotated margin, the late Jacques Derrida (1930–2004) includes a definition of *catachresis* as if it were a dictionary entry: "Catachresis . . . n. 1. Trope wherein a word is diverted from its proper sense and is taken up in common language to designate another thing with some analogy to the object initially expressed . . . 2. Musical term. Harsh and unfamiliar dissonance."[15] The Latin for catachresis, *abusio*, reflects a term's misuse or strained use of language, as does the Greek, *kata* against, *khresthai*, to use. Catachresis is constructed like metaphor but, by contrast, initially fails to bridge the gap between two dimensions of meaning; like a non-lubricated analogy. Just as the range between metaphor and catachresis is a matter of degree, Dylan's success with it is as well.

In *Tarantula*, headings such as "Pointless like a Witch," "Sand in the Mouth of the Movie Star," and "Pocketful of Scoundrel" seem to be part of the impenetrable language throughout this first Dylan publication. Dylan uses something

---

[15] Jacques Derrida, *Glas* (Lincoln: University of Nebraska Press, 1974), p. 2.

like catachresis in the juxtaposition of phrases or sentences that don't seem to go together while in their suspension of meaning, having the right aesthetic impact, pushing to the foreground mood and atmosphere. This results in switching vantage points and perspectives too quickly for too much thought. We think there is something musical here, like moving from a refrain to a chorus, and it is also transformative, moving from the everyday to something new and other. The transformative power of music is a Nietzschean theme, and in *Tarantula* we find an appeal to aretha along these telling lines: "so sing Aretha . . . sing mainstream into orbit! sing the cowbells home! sing misty . . . it then must be time for you to rest & learn new songs . . . forgiving nothing for you have done nothing & make love to the noble scrubwoman" (pp. 10–11). The transfigurative power of art in both Nietzsche and Dylan is particularly acute where ethical and aesthetic values are often conflated.

So then, Dylan's *Tarantula* is a minor epic in the language of dirty reality. It's thinly framed by the realm of "aretha/ crystal jukebox queen of hymn & him" but it is a world of in-your-face audacity, "a cut-throat high and low." The narrator in *Tarantula* offers scenarios with a kind of unmindful flow told from a non-tuistic (not caring much about others) point of view. The distance created by the narrator between himself and those encountered approximates his distance from the reader, who also feels something of Dylan's venomous bite.

Tarantula's End

One final remark and this may be especially relevant in light of Dylan's *Chronicles*. About three-fourths of the way through *Tarantula* the writing changes: the segments become longer and, we think, more coherent. In one of these final pieces, Dylan writes about a dream he had, which parallels an incident that happened the afternoon of that dream. Awake, Dylan is in a forest playing his guitar, and someone says it is three o'clock. Later on he reads in the paper that a three o'clock tenement fire caused nineteen deaths. In Dylan's dream, he is playing the guitar, in the same forest. And, in the dream, there is a blazing tenement. Oddly he adds, "it was not worth analyzing as nothing is worth analyzing." While the tenement is burning, the dreamer becomes transported and so too does the tenement so that upon their temporal juxtaposition, the dreamer continues to sing in front of the raging fire but is unable to do anything because "we were not in the same Space."

Dylan comments on this dream: "i could not feel any guilt about just standing there singing for as i said i was picked up & moved there not by my own free will but rather by some unbelievable force" (p. 107). Awake, he tells his friend Justine about this dream, and she assures him that he's only human and that his not feeling guilty is okay. Dylan then adds, "i got very drunk that afternoon & a mysterious confusion entered into my body." Since we don't need a weatherman to say which way the wind blows, we'll leave *Tarantula* right here.[16]

---

[16] We would like to thank Christopher Ricks, Theodore Gracyk, Ruvik Danieli, Georgia Riepe and Peter Vernezze for their helpful comments. Gracyk reminded us of Dylan's mention of Nietzsche in his song *Joey* and Ricks mentioned to us the *Advice to Geraldine*, among other things.

15

When I Paint My Masterpiece: What Sort of Artist Is Bob Dylan?

THEODORE GRACYK

All art constantly aspires towards the condition of music
. . . In music, then, rather than in poetry, is to be found the
true type or measure of perfected art . . . Life itself is conceived as a sort of listening—listening to music, or the reading
of Bandello's novels, to the sound of water, to time as it flies.

—WALTER PATER[1]

It was an artistic challenge to see if great art can be done on
a jukebox . . . [Dylan] proved it can.

—ALLEN GINSBERG[2]

What Makes Someone an Artist?

In 1997, the John F. Kennedy Center for the Performing Arts
selected Bob Dylan as one of the year's five honorees, placing
him in the company of past recipients Aaron Copland, Leonard
Bernstein, Arthur Miller, Fred Astaire, and Martha Graham.
Dylan was now a certified as a *real* artist, not just a pop musician. The status of artist may seem trivial in an age when the
word is applied to anyone who makes a record or has a bit part
in a movie, but the Kennedy Center Honors were established to

---

[1] Walter Pater, "The School of Giorgione," *The Renaissance: Studies in Art and
Poetry*, Library Edition (London: Macmillan, 1922), pp. 135, 139, 151.
[2] Quoted in Ralph J. Gleason, "The Children's Crusade," in Craig McGregor,
ed., *Bob Dylan: A Retrospective*, (New York: Morrow, 1972), p.185; the essay
originally appeared in *Ramparts*, 1966.

recognize ongoing contributions to American culture through the performing arts. But what additional status do we assign to Dylan when we say that he's an artist, beyond whatever is covered by identifying him as a songwriter and professional musician? I will review three ideas about art and artists that might explain what it means to say that Dylan is an artist.

The verdict on Dylan, by the way, is hardly unanimous. At the height of his 1960s fame, the *New York Times* asked a number of poets and poetry teachers about Dylan. The responses were uniformly negative.[3]

More recently, classical composer Ned Rorem condemned Dylan's music and performances as "beneath contempt . . . I find him utterly devoid of anything."[4]

Some people have difficulty seeing the problem that I am confronting. But ask some random people what carpenters' wives and mathematicians have in common. Chances are that most will be confused, or will think you're telling a riddle. To a Dylan fan, the answer is obvious. According to "Tangled Up in Blue," they're both "people we used to know." Someone who has a lot of exposure to art might assume that it's obvious what constitutes art and who counts as an artist, but perhaps there is no tighter link between the various people we call "artist" than among "people we used to know."

To put the same point another way, some fishermen and some comic book collectors are hobbyists, but some are not. Some fishermen fish for a living. Some comic book collectors buy them as an investment. So there is no logical connection among these categories. There is a parallel issue with songwriting, music performance, and art. Some music performers are artists. But some are not, a fact easily confirmed by attending a music recital by a class of first graders.

Dylan is certainly aware of the problem I am raising. Many Dylan fans know of the 1965 interview in which he was asked if he thinks of himself more as a poet or as a singer. He responded, "I think of myself more as a song and dance man."[5]

---

[3] See "Is Bob Dylan the Greatest Poet in the United States Today?", in McGregor, p. 167; the piece originally appeared in 1965.
[4] Jay Nordlinger, "The World of Ned Rorem," *National Review Online* (February 12th, 2002), http://www.nationalreview.com/nordlinger/nordlinger021203.asp.
[5] San Francisco Press Conference, December 3rd, 1965.

More recently, Dylan remarked that what he does puts him in the same category as "the amusement business, along with theme parks, popcorn and horror shows." Most of what takes place at concerts, he complains, "has nothing to do with music."[6] Dylan knows that not everything he does makes him an artist.

As recently as three hundred years ago, no one thought that painters, sculptors, architects, composers, and poets should be grouped together as five species of a common kind, artist.[7] Painters and sculptors and musicians were recognized as skilled artisans, on a par with cooks and masons. Some of them were singled out for their genius and special gifts. Although the Renaissance was an important stage in the development of cultural respect for visual art and artists, Renaissance opinion did not embrace the idea of a common purpose that included music and poetry. So no era before the eighteenth century would have regarded Dylan's "Italian poet from the thirteenth century" as a peer of visual artists such as Michelangelo or Picasso. Dylan's Italian poet would not have recognized Dylan as an artist.

What occurred during the lifetimes of George Washington and Benjamin Franklin to encourage us, today, to treat a singer-songwriter as an artist? The crucial event was the development of a general theory of art, one that recognizes practitioners of different crafts as pursuing a common goal. A general theory of art allows us to say that some songwriters are merely songwriters. Others, like Dylan, are artists.

Philosophers have debated about the nature of art since the eighteenth century. For two millennia, philosophers had emphasized ideal knowledge, devoid of any perceptual dimension. Then the scientific revolution made it clear that the five senses are indispensable for knowledge. Philosophers responded by developing a new topic, aesthetics, to explore perceptual knowledge. A simultaneous explosion of artistic styles and methods redirected aesthetics into the modern field of philosophy of art.

The biggest problem with explaining why Dylan is an artist and not *merely* a songwriter and singer is that there are many

---

[6] "Tell It Like It Is," *USA Today* (September 9th, 2001), http://www.usatoday.com/life/music/2001-09-10-dylan-quotes.htm.
[7] Paul Oskar Kristeller, "The Modern System of the Arts: A Study in the History of Aesthetics," *Journal of the History of Ideas* 12:4 (1951), pp. 496–527.

competing explanations of art and artistry. A recent textbook in the philosophy of art, Thomas Wartenberg's *The Nature of Art,* distinguishes twenty-eight different attempts to define art! Unable to survey so many theories, I am going to concentrate on three widely accepted theories: expression theory, formalism, and Immanuel Kant's theory of genius.

Artists and Expression

Poetry is the spontaneous overflow of powerful feelings: it takes its origin from emotion recollected in tranquility.

—WILLIAM WORDSWORTH, Preface to *Lyrical Ballads* (1802)

One familiar and popular view is that artists have a talent for expressing emotion. This activity is regarded as valuable when it calls attention to emotions that we would otherwise suppress or deny. A great deal of writing about Dylan assumes that he is an expressive artist. This approach also tells us that some musical activity is not art, either because the musician has nothing to express, or because there is an emotion but it is not successfully revealed.

One thing that might encourage us to apply expression theory to Dylan is that it says that ugliness doesn't matter. Sincerity and authenticity matter. This neutralizes the objection that Dylan can't sing, or that he sounds like "a dog with his leg caught in barbed wire."[8]

Expression does not require beauty, grace, or even tunefulness. Emotion is what matters. Joan Baez objected to the raw and aggressive treatment that Dylan gave "Lay Lady Lay" during his 1974 tour, reportedly dismissing it as "nasty."[9]

She may have disliked its emotional reinvention, but according to the expression theory, a "nasty" emotion is just as legitimate as an uplifting one.[10]

---

[8] Attributed to a "Missouri folk singer," this frequently quoted description originates in Nat Hentoff, "The Playboy Interview: Bob Dylan," in McGregor, p. 125. The interview was originally published in *Playboy* (March 1966).

[9] Quoted in Doug Patt, "In the Courtyard of the Jester," in Bill Yenne, ed., *One Foot on the Highway: Bob Dylan on Tour* (San Francisco: Klonh, 1974), p. 18.

[10] Expression theory often limits good art to expression of uplifting or positive emotions. In the version defended by Leo Tolstoy, Dylan's best music would

According to the expression theory, Dylan is an artist whenever he exposes his soul. On this model, "Neighborhood Bully" is better than "Lily, Rosemary, and the Jack of Hearts," an assessment that I'm not sure I want to endorse.

We must remember that a theory that praises some work will condemn some, too. There are times when Dylan is going through the motions, and fails as an artist. Consider Greil Marcus's lengthy, brutal review of *Self Portrait* in *Rolling Stone*. Tracks are dismissed with comments of "lifeless," "product," and "fake." "Let It Be Me" is criticized by observing, "For all of the emotion usually found in his singing, there is virtually none here." But "Copper Kettle" is singled out for praise, as "the only time" on *Self Portrait* that his singing makes "room for expression and emotion."[11]

Clinton Heylin and Paul Williams also employ expression theory in their many writings on Dylan. Williams's three volumes of *Bob Dylan: Performing Artist* use expression as a measure of artistry on almost every page. In one passage, Williams praises Dylan's *Real Live* performance of "Girl from the North Country" as "a wonderfully intimate performance." Yet he also thinks that it is something less than art: "It is not, I might argue, great art, because although it is heartfelt it does not go down to the deep place where new and unexpected feelings burst through."[12]

Here, Williams adopts the high standard for art defended by philosopher R.G. Collingwood in *The Principles of Art*. According to Collingwood, artistry is imaginative activity that makes us conscious of our emotions. The expression theory justifies the idea that Dylan, as the expressive voice of his generation, is a great artist.

But must artists express their *own* emotions? If music is a vehicle for expression, why can't composers use the media of music and words to express emotions that they have not per-

---

be the more positive songs and performances of his "Christian" period, such as "Pressing On" and "What Can I Do for You?"

[11] Opening with the question, "What is this shit?" the review is reprinted in *The Rolling Stone Record Review* (New York: Pocket Books, 1971), pp. 514–530; quotations from pages 517 and 522, respectively.

[12] Paul Williams, *Bob Dylan: Performing Artist The Middle Years: 1974–1986* (Novato: Underwood Miller, 1992), pp. 253–54.

sonally experienced? If they start with their own emotions, must they be honest in expressing them? T.S. Eliot proposes that a poet should take the personal and, in giving it some objective externalization, render it impersonal. Art demands some degree of "depersonalization," Eliot argues. Artistic success requires "continual self-sacrifice, a continual extinction of personality."[13]

Eliot seems to mean that art that is uniquely about the artist will not express anything to the audience. If it remains too personal, no one else can grasp it.

Blood on the Tracks offers a test case for deciding where one stands on this issue. Clinton Heylin's many writings on Dylan endorse Collingwood's ideas about expression. Consequently, Heylin contends that the unreleased first version of *Blood* is superior to the released album. In re-recording six tracks, Dylan made the songs "less personal . . . compromising his art to tone down his previously naked pain."[14]

Heylin even claims that the remake of "Tangled Up in Blue" succeeds because it "clearly retained its emotional connection" to Dylan's personal life.[15]

But is it that, or is it because Dylan took Kevin Odegard's advice to move it from the key of E to A? Forcing Dylan to reach for the notes, this *musical* alteration contributes a great deal to Dylan's sense of emotional urgency. Bill Berg's drumming and Billy Peterson's bass line also contribute to the expressive character of the performance. Like the decision to play it in the key of A, neither of these changes from the New York sessions originates in Dylan's personal life.

If one dogmatically insists that expression is central to artistry, one might agree with Heylin that the released *Blood on the Tracks* album is an artistic travesty. However, fans who've heard the "original" album usually regard the reworked, less personal version as the superior one. Dylan's most personal work is not always his musically richest and most interesting.

---

[13] T.S. Eliot, "Tradition and the Individual Talent," in *Selected Prose of T.S. Eliot* (New York: Harcourt, Brace, 1956), p. 40.

[14] Clinton Heylin, *Bob Dylan Behind the Shades: A Biography* (New York: Summit, 1991), p. 246.

[15] Clinton Heylin, *Bob Dylan: The Recording Sessions 1960–1994* (New York: St. Martin's Griffin, 1995), p. 107.

Live concerts provide another reason to wonder if expression and artistry are tightly bound. Consider Dylan's 1964 Hallowe'en concert, on *The Bootleg Series, volume 6*. Between songs, Dylan is almost performing stand-up comedy. Introducing the as-yet-unreleased "Gates of Eden," Dylan says, "This is called 'A Sacrilegious Lullaby in D Minor.' [Dylan laughs and strums his guitar] That's the D minor." The mocking introductions seldom match the mood of the songs. Surely we do not assume a supernatural power to change emotions on demand. Do we explain this disparity by invoking Wordsworth's Romantic doctrine, saying that Dylan *remembers* his earlier emotions when he sings? But this move introduces a gap between expressing emotions (when composing) and creating music that seems expressive of emotion (when performing).

If live performance allows Dylan to conjure up an emotion that he does not currently have, why can't he do the same when composing? But then his knowledge of craft should allow him to effectively convey emotions he has never had. Expression theory does not offer much guidance in separating the genuine from the fake, the good from the bad.

Artists and Form

What got me into the whole thing in the beginning wasn't song-writing . . . What interested me was being a musician. The singer was important and so was the song. But being a musician was always first and foremost in the back of my mind.

—Dylan[16]

There's no rule. That's what makes it so attractive.

—Dylan on songwriting[17]

The greatest obstacles to recognizing Dylan as an artist arise from the idea that artists create original, beautiful designs that provide pleasure. Biographical facts about the artist are not relevant to its success or failure. Music is no better or worse for

---

[16] Quoted in Paul Zollo, *Songwriters on Songwriting*, Expanded Edition (New York: Da Capo, 1997), p. 83.
[17] Quoted in Zollo, p.72.

reflecting the place or time or circumstances of its creation, be it Vienna in the eighteenth century (Mozart's symphonies) or New York in the 1960s (Dylan's "Talkin' World War III Blues"). Nor is it better or worse because it does or doesn't reflect the composer's own life. A good work transcends its origins. An artwork's merits and flaws reside in its design.

Because this approach emphasizes the creation of design or structure, it is called "formalism." Nineteenth-century artists and critics who favored expressive values attacked it as an old-fashioned, restrictive endorsement of the "classical" world of ancient Greece and Rome. So it is sometimes called "classicism" to contrast it with the more modern sensibility that emphasizes individual expression.

Writers and critics who concentrate on Dylan's verbal skills usually subscribe to classicism. Any Dylan fan who's taken a look at Michael Gray's *Song and Dance Man* or Christopher Ricks's *Dylan's Visions of Sin* knows what I mean. Dylan is praised as a master of syntax, rhyme, and patterning. He knows just which melodies (or adapted melodies) and meters will set off interesting emphases in the words. As Ricks puts it, "Rhymes and rhythms and cadences will be what brings a poem home to us."[18] Dylan is an artist because he combines everyday and inherited language into intricate shapes, and because he continually finds fresh patterns of American English to refresh tired expressions. Even seemingly simple songs, such as "One Too Many Mornings," turn out to be crammed with interesting crosscurrents and verbal transferences.[19]

But a critical perspective that praises Dylan's verbal skills does not have kind words for Dylan as a performer. Classicism regards performance as mere servant of the work: a good musical performance displays the merits of the musical composition. From this perspective, we should not be surprised that the Byrds' splendid cover version of "Mr. Tambourine Man" was more popular than Dylan's acoustic version. If we ignore the lyrics, many of Dylan's compositions are relatively simple, with serviceable but undistinguished melodies. Consider the famous breakthrough albums of the 1960s that feature "that thin, that

---

[18] Christopher Ricks, *Dylan's Visions of Sin* (New York: HarperCollins, 2003), p. 31.
[19] Ricks, pp. 427–28.

wild mercury sound," namely *Bringing It All Back Home*, *Highway 61 Revisited*, and *Blonde on Blonde*.[20] Most of the songs are extraordinarily predictable blues tunes.

It might be tempting to praise Dylan the performer as an expressive artist, and Dylan the composer as a classicist. But two obstacles block this escape route. First, we've already seen that *Blood on the Tracks* is a failure according to the expressive theory, so we should not trust that theory to explain why his performances are valuable. The second reason is historical. Romanticism justified using poetry for personal expression by attacking classicism. Classicists understood that artists achieve formal excellence only by downplaying the excesses of real emotional expression. If classicism praises Dylan as a composer, highly expressive performances would require Dylan, as performer, to violate his goals as a composer. Dylan as classicist would be at war with Dylan the performer.

We will have better luck if we go right to the compositions, and admit that most of Dylan's music is pretty simple. So simple, in fact, that his recording sessions are infamous for his expectation that other musicians can play new songs without rehearsals and without discussing the musical arrangements. As a musical performer, Dylan doesn't seek the perfection of classicism. He seeks the kind of formal success that Ted Gioia calls "a different type of form," one that embraces "an aesthetic of imperfection, one which accepts [the] human element in art."[21]

Classicism demands structural perfection, best accomplished by faithfully executing structurally balanced compositions that map out the details of each performance. But instead of treating musical works as blueprints that control performances, the blues and jazz traditions employ a "retrospective method" of composing-while-playing. There is less interest in executing what has been mapped out than there is in seeing

---

[20] Dylan quoted in Ron Rosenbaum, "The Playboy Interview: Bob Dylan," *Playboy* (March 1978), p. 74. Available at http://www.interferenza.com/bcs/interw/play78.htm.

[21] Ted Gioia, *The Imperfect Art: Reflections on Jazz and Modern Culture* (New York: Oxford University Press, 1988), pp. 59 and 68, respectively. While Gioia is interested in jazz improvisation, he concedes that this type of form is not restricted to jazz.

what can be accomplished in the act of playing. In other words, you don't just play a song. You play with it.

The retrospective method of converting simple form into complex performance is Dylan's preferred performance standard. In the early years, it appeared in his harmonica solos and his between-song stage patter. Dylan's decision to go "electric" in 1965 is less significant for amplification than for his inauguration of an ongoing reliance on other musicians' unrehearsed contributions. The object is to collectively fill in a simple structure, letting details emerge from the spontaneous decisions of the players. The price to pay is that many performances include missed cues, unfocused instrumental passages, and singing that seems a mere afterthought. Dylan's performances became increasingly haphazard. But at their best, they are unconventional and riveting. The price to pay is *Knocked Out Loaded* and *Dylan and the Dead*. The reward is *Blonde on Blonde* and *"Love and Theft."*

Artists, Meaning, and Genius

If you want to send a message, call Western Union.

—film producer SAM GOLDWYN

You've got to respect other people's right to also have a message themselves. Myself, what I'm going to do is rent Town Hall and put about thirty Western Union boys on the bill. I mean, then there'll *really* be some messages. People will be able to come and hear more messages than they've ever heard before in their life.

—BOB DYLAN, 1966[22]

If Dylan's performances are best approached in terms of the aesthetics of imperfection, and if the merits of the songs are not exhausted by expression theory, we must consider the relation of form to content in Dylan's body of work. The aesthetics of imperfection assigns more value to musical play than to fixed design. Does the same principle extend to the interplay of words and music in Dylan's work? What kind of artist is Dylan if he is also interested in playing with the meanings of words?

---

[22] Quoted in Hentoff, "The Playboy Interview," in McGregor, p. 133.

We will want an account that does not treat "play" as trivial entertainment. One such theory of art is philosopher Immanuel Kant's emphasis on the free play of imagination and understanding in artistic production.[23]

On this theory, artists engage with ideas. The artistry displayed in presenting ideas will be one of two types: mannerism or genius. Dylan's "original" songs and debut album are mannerist exercises—"Talkin' New York" and "Song to Woody" closely imitate the models that inspire him. This stage is inevitable, for it provides knowledge of form and design and so educates the artist's critical abilities or taste. But genius moves beyond what "diligence and learning" can provide. The artistic genius transforms an existing tradition through an infusion of unpredictable originality. A successful work prompts the audience's imagination "to spread over a multitude of kindred presentations," so that the work is rich in associations but cannot be encapsulated under just one concept or under any one paraphrase. In short, genius requires a natural talent for expressing "ineffable" ideas through the play of imagination.[24]

Although they're cut from the same cloth of Christian righteousness, the train metaphor at the center of "Slow Train" opens it to multiple associations and so elevates it above the hectoring of "Gotta Serve Somebody." The musical feeling of train building speed strengthens the metaphor of "Slow Train." The preachy musical cadences of "Gotta Serve Somebody" leave it one-dimensional.

Dylan has said that words give songs their purpose.[25] But it does not follow that each set of words has only a definite purpose that must be the same in every performance or the same for every listener. Literal meaning and passion are less important than finding fresh combinations of sound, word arrangement, and imagery, so that their mutual interactions stir the imagination. Parallels and analogies in other topics enrich a central theme or message. "Knockin' on Heaven's Door" and

---

[23] My summary downplays Kant's classicism and emphasis on beauty. Kant's theory of art is in his *Critique of Judgment*, sections 43–54. Many good translations are available. I have used the James Creed Meredith translation (Oxford: Oxford University Press, 1911).

[24] Kant, section 49.

[25] Rosenbaum, "The Playboy Interview," p. 74.

"Tryin' to Get to Heaven" are songs about impending death. Yet neither actually mentions death. In each song the musical line and central verbal metaphor invites the listener to consider heaven and death in contrasting ways. "Heaven's Door" relies on the metaphor of a closed door, and a desire to open it. The chorus has a hopeful feeling. "Tryin' to Get to Heaven" alters the door metaphor—the door is open, but closing. The chorus sounds rueful. If we take "Not Dark Yet" as yet another meditation on death, the subject is transformed again. Dylan uses the familiar subjects of a door and twilight to elucidate one of life's mysteries.

This approach implies that "Desolation Row" and "Visions of Johanna" are superior to the didactic "fingerpointing" and apparent sincerity of songs like "Masters of War" and "Positively 4th Street." It endorses the long-standing view that *Bringing It All Back Home* represents a breakthrough in Dylan's artistry. Yet this theory cannot regard the songs of 1965 and 1966 as unqualified successes. Ellen Willis was correct to observe, in 1967, that much of Dylan's writing was sloppy and undisciplined.[26]

Artistic genius, warned Kant, always runs the risk of generating nonsense. Originality must be balanced with good taste and critical insight that will constrain and shape the excesses of genius. *John Wesley Harding* is the first set of songs in which Dylan consistently balances genius and taste. Dylan's new economy of language invites us to ponder every turn of phrase. While there have been lapses since 1968, Dylan has been surprisingly consistent in controlling his imaginative excesses by anchoring the words in strongly traditional music.

Last Thoughts

> The human element is essential to a masterpiece. The artist must be deeply involved in the understanding of his fellow men.
>
> —KENNETH CLARK[27]

Some theories define art without telling us why we should value what artists do. These theories aim to classify without evaluat-

---

[26] Ellen Willis, "Dylan," in McGregor, pp. 233–34.
[27] Kenneth Clark, *What Is a Masterpiece?* (New York: Thames and Hudson, 1979), p. 12.

ing. I have concentrated on theories that derive evaluations from claims about the nature of art and artists. However, none of the three theories applauds the full range of Dylan's composing and performing activities. In the evaluative sense of explaining why Dylan's artistic activity makes him an *important* or *great* artist, Kant's theory of genius is the most satisfactory of the three that I have explored. There are other important theories of art, some nearly as popular as the three I've selected. Each provides a different lens for exploring different facets of Dylan's career.

16

You Who Philosophize Dylan: The Quarrel between Philosophy and Poetry in the Songs of Bob Dylan

KEVIN L. STOEHR

In a collection of essays that attempt to show how Bob Dylan and his songs can be used to discuss philosophy, it may not be out of place to ask whether one *ought to* adopt a philosophical approach *at all* when it comes to this prolific wordsmith. What are we doing, exactly, when we attempt to "philosophize Dylan"? Philosophers, of course, like to pose questions about the meaning and value of what they are doing. By philosophizing about philosophy itself, philosophers seem to reassure themselves that they are, in fact, doing philosophy. But what are we doing precisely when we attempt to philosophize about this legendary troubadour of our times?

We are searching, no doubt, for meaning and value in his life and lyrics. But what needs saying beyond the life and lyrics themselves? Philosophy, as the ancient Greek thinker Aristotle tells us, is a *search* initiated by a sense of wonder and a desire to understand. Yet Dylan asks, as if in retort: "But how long, babe / Can you search for what's not lost?" ("I'll Keep It with Mine"). And how long must we ponder before understanding, for example, what the jelly-faced woman means when she utters, "Jeeze / I can't find my knees?" ("Visions of Johanna").

Does philosophy really have any place at all when it comes to an appreciative understanding of Dylan's musical *poetry*? For surely what Dylan does and has been doing for some time qualifies as a form of poetry. As the celebrated literary critic and Dylan scholar Christopher Ricks puts it in his recent book *Dylan's Visions of Sin*: "The case for denying Dylan the title of poet could not summarily, if at all, be made good by any open-minded close attention to the words and his ways with them."[1] This gets to the heart of a perennial question about the relationship or tension between philosophy and poetry. Some have called it a "quarrel." Thinkers ranging from Plato in ancient times to Martin Heidegger in the twentieth century have addressed this relationship in one way or another. In Plato's famous dialogue *The Republic*, his main character Socrates imagines the need to banish from his ideal "city in speech" those poets who appeal to irrational desires rather than dedicate themselves to the quest for knowledge and truth. (Plato may have forgotten that he himself was very much a poet at times, especially when it came to creating myths, though he was a strictly philosophical poet and mythmaker.) In Boethius's classic work *The Consolation of Philosophy*, our author from the Middle Ages depicts his own final days in a locked prison cell far from his home in Rome. He banishes the Muses of Poetry so that he might converse with his newly arrived guest, Lady Philosophy, about such themes as happiness, fate, providence, evil, freedom, and God. And yet the poetic muses never truly depart his chamber, ironically, since the entire "dialogue" is a *satura*, a combination of prose and poetry. Poetry remains with Boethius until his dying day, we might infer, or at least until the *Consolation*'s conclusion. And in Dante's *La Vita Nuova*, to take yet another example of the relation or tension in question, the Italian bard presents inspired poetry in honor of his beloved, Beatrice, while interjecting philosophical explanations of this very attempt to put his love for her beauty into words. So what tells us more about his love: the poetry or the philosophy? And why is philosophical prose needed here at all, amidst the fragments of a very spiritual and personal love poem?

Do philosophy and poetry reside on the peaks of two different mountains, so to speak, or do they help to form the same mountain, like layers of ice and stone? And even if they are somehow set apart from one another, may there not be a bridge, no matter how rickety, that still connects them? Most particularly, how do these two dimensions of human expression relate to one another when considering the songs of Bob Dylan?

---

[1] Christopher Ricks, *Dylan's Vision of Sin* (New York: HarperCollins, 2003), p. 19.

Just Like a Woman's Intuition

At the conclusion of his 1986 *Rolling Stone* interview with Mikal Gilmore, Dylan appears to lower his public mask ever so slightly. He proclaims in a rare burst of self-analysis:

> See, I've always been just about being an individual, with an individual point of view. If I've been about anything, it's probably that, and to let some people know that it's possible to do the impossible . . . If I've ever had anything to tell anybody, it's that: You can do the impossible. Anything is possible. And that's it. No more.[2]

An individual is someone who cannot be neatly classified or categorized because he or she cannot be easily dissected or analyzed, divided into definable parts. The individual is, first and foremost, a being-unto-itself, a unique whole: something undivided, according to the Latin root term ("individuum").

It goes without saying that Bob Dylan, as unique and original and unpredictable as any artist-entertainer before or after him, is an *individual* in the genuine sense of the word. (Which prompts the question: Why do we tend so often to say what goes without saying? Poets tend to do this at times, but so do philosophers.) One can easily define Dylan as a *poet* (even though he is so much more), but one might be wary of calling Bob Dylan a "philosopher" (whatever that may mean). After all, Dylan proclaimed in a 1995 *USA Today* interview not long after his MTV *Unplugged* performance:

> As you get older, you get smarter and that can hinder you because you try to gain control over the creative impulse. Creativity is not like a freight train going down the tracks. It's something that has to be caressed and treated with a great deal of respect. If your mind is intellectually in the way, it will stop you. You've got to program your brain not to think too much.[3]

But how does one intend to "program" one's mind "not to think too much" without thinking a good deal about the benefits and

---

[2] Mikal Gilmore, "Positively Dylan," in Carl Benson, ed., *The Bob Dylan Companion: Four Decades of Commentary*, (New York: Schirmer, 1998), p. 198.

[3] Edna Gundersen, "Dylan on Dylan: 'Unplugged' and the Birth of a Song," in *Dylan Companion*, p. 225.

dangers of thinking too much? The great irony is that Dylan tends to wax philosophical here in his very attempt to discount the intellectual-philosophical dimension of his own creative drive. This is a very "Nietzschean" tendency, one might say, in that the famous nineteenth-century German philosopher Friedrich Nietzsche (1844–1900) attacked the traditional enterprise of philosophy while nonetheless attempting to give philosophical reasons for his attack. To say something critical of the act of saying something philosophical, one cannot help (it would seem) saying something philosophical.

Therein lies the irony—both Nietzsche and Dylan are master ironists, it goes without saying once again—and the only way out of the vicious circle is, perhaps, to criticize philosophy from somewhere beyond philosophy itself. From the realm of poetry, perhaps?

But does Dylan really "side with" poetry "over" philosophy? We know that *philosophy*, whatever else it may be, is intrinsically concerned with the art of rational *thinking*. How much thinking does Dylan actually put into the lyrics of his songs? How do the philosophical and poetic dimensions of Dylan's lyrics stand in relation to one another? (We are suspending here a discussion of the actual *music* that accompanies Dylan's lyrics, not to mention his *voice*).

In a 1985 interview with Robert Hilburn of the *Los Angeles Times*, Dylan tells us about the creation of one of his most popular songs, "Forever Young": "I wrote [it] . . . thinking about one of my boys and not wanting to be too sentimental. The lines came to me, they were done in a minute . . . the song wrote itself."[4] And as he tells Hilburn in 1992, in reference to his superb spiritual meditation "Every Grain of Sand": "That's an excellent song, very painless to write . . . It took like twelve seconds—or that's how it felt."[5] He echoes this reference to the same song in his liner notes to the *Biograph* collection: "That was an inspired song that came to me. It wasn't really too difficult. I felt like I was just putting words down that were coming from somewhere else." And as Dylan tells us when discussing his song "Caribbean Wind" (outtake from the album *Shot of*

---

[4] Robert Hilburn, "Bob Dylan: Still A-Changin'," in *Dylan Companion*, p. 204.
[5] Robert Hilburn, "Forever Dylan: On the Never-Ending Tour with Rock's Greatest Poet," in *Dylan Companion*, p. 220.

Love), from the same notes: "That one I couldn't quite grasp what it was about after I finished it. Sometimes you'll write something to be very inspired."[6]

Like the true poet that he is, Dylan believes that when it comes to the construction of his lyrics (and certainly the creation of the music itself, we might assume), the power of immediate intuition counts far more than the categorizing and ordering power of the intellect. He tells Hilburn in the 1992 interview, concerning his classic "Just Like a Woman": "That's a hard song to pin down. It's another one of those that you can sing a thousand times and still ask what is it about, but you know there's a real feeling there."[7] He confesses to Hilburn in 1997, while referring to Neil Young in the sprawling epic "Highlands" from his recent *Time Out of Mind* album: "It's anything you want it to be. [smiles] I don't give too much thought to individual lines. If I thought about them in any kind of deep way, maybe I wouldn't use them because I'd always be second-guessing myself. I learned a long time ago to trust my intuition."[8] And in regard to his song "Señor (Tales of Yankee Power)," Dylan declares (also in the *Biograph* notes): "[S]ometimes you'll write something because you've lived something and you someplace along the line say to yourself, 'Why am I writing this? It will never be as good as I lived it.' But then it sometimes turns out better than what you've lived . . . it's bigger and less trashy."[9] Intuition, of course, is the inner illumination that derives directly from *lived experience* rather than from rigorous reflection.

The poet, it may hopefully be agreed, depends far more upon immediate intuition than the philosopher. Or, to put it more safely, the poet is happy to remain at the level of intuition—to hover playfully around what is immediately given by the muses, so to speak—rather than to transcend that level through rational explanation, analysis, and evaluation.

Like all great poets, Dylan attempts in many of his songs to somehow "say the unsayable"—to capture a vague mood or some surreal series of fleeting images, yet in static, generic words. The attempt must necessarily fail due to the limits of lan-

---

[6] *Biograph*, liner notes.
[7] Hilburn, *Dylan Companion*, p. 221.
[8] Robert Hilburn, "Reborn Again," in *Dylan Companion*, p. 250.
[9] *Biograph*, liner notes.

guage (and so not just *anything* is possible, despite what Dylan told Gilmore—especially when it comes to the art of "saying"). And yet it is the poet's very *attempt* that we salute, especially if it affords our minds and imaginations new vistas or horizons.

In his hymn to hopelessness from the album *Time Out of Mind*, a song entitled "Not Dark Yet," Dylan sings in his raspy croak: "She put down in writing what was in her mind." The poet's endeavor to do the same—an endeavor that is sometimes frustrating, sometimes thrilling—is captured to a degree by the following statement, which is Dylan's own brief distillation of his unconscious creative yearnings. As he said to Ron Rosenbaum in a 1978 *Playboy* interview, concerning his ability on the *Blonde on Blonde* album to realize some of his deepest musical intentions: "It's that thin, that wild mercury sound. It's metallic and bright gold, with whatever that conjures up. That's my sound. I haven't been able to succeed in getting it all the time."[10]

And yet, as with any complex artist who expresses inner contradictions and nuances, Dylan can not be pegged simply as "anti-philosophical" or even "anti-conceptual" in his regular reliance upon immediate intuition and unconscious mood or imagery. Again, he is a true individual in that he cannot be categorized or dissected neatly. Dylan sometimes attempts (though rarely) to articulate an intention for a song that is as *conceptual* as it is intuitive. For instance, in the *Biograph* notes he discusses the fundamental idea behind the complex lyrical tapestry that is "Tangled Up in Blue":

> I guess I was just trying to make it like a painting where you can see the different parts but then you also see the whole of it. With that particular song, that's what I was trying to do . . . with the concept of time, and the way the characters change from the first person to the third person, and you're never quite sure if the third person is talking or the first person is talking. But as you look at the whole thing it really doesn't matter.[11]

To say that Dylan is not a philosopher *per se* does not mean necessarily that many of his *songs* are not philosophical, if we are to understand "philosophical" here in the rather general

---

[10] *Biograph*, liner notes.
[11] *Biograph*, liner notes.

sense of "making us think deeply." In terms of the listener's reception of a Dylan song rather than in terms of Dylan's own intentions in creating it, many of his songs certainly serve effectively in provoking reflection of a philosophical sort. To take but two clear examples: "Every Grain of Sand" impels its thoughtful listener to consider themes of destiny, chance, freedom, and God, while "The Lonesome Death of Hattie Carroll" evokes questions about human evil and injustice.

Nostalgia and Nihilism

The legendary German poet Friedrich Hölderlin (1770–1843) was, in his youthful days as a seminary student in Tübingen, close friends with two of German Idealism's philosophical giants: Friedrich Schelling (1775–1854) and Georg Hegel (1770–1831). All three were concerned with, among other things, the capacity of philosophical thought to grasp the way things really are.

Before dedicating himself strictly to poetry (and then eventually succumbing to a long period of mental illness), Hölderlin also exercised his considerable talents as a philosopher. So it's not surprising to find him posing a very philosophical question about the purpose or function of a poet, particularly during an age in which the very idea of purpose or function had been put into question by speculative thinkers: "[A]nd what are poets for in a destitute time?" ("Bread and Wine"). We are led to wonder if poetry really has a unique purpose or function at all, since Hölderlin tells us elsewhere that "man" (*all* humans, it would seem) somehow "dwells poetically" in the world: "Full of merit, yet poetically, man / Dwells on this earth."

There can be no doubt that Bob Dylan is a poet in the genuine sense of that term. His way of "dwelling in the world" is poetic through and through, given the quality and quantity of his output over the decades. But what *kind* of a poet is he, and does he practice the type of poetry that lends itself to philosophical analysis or interpretation? Or is he perhaps the best kind of poet—the kind that is so *unkind* to the philosopher because he can not be pinned down by types or categories or kinds? Does Dylan "dwell poetically" in a way that many of us do not? And does "poetic dwelling" require philosophical thinking in any way?

Dylan appears to answer this last question in the negative by way of his "11 Outlined Epitaphs," which form the liner notes to his early album *The Times They Are A'Changin'*: "a word, a tune, a story, a line / keys in the wind t' unlock my mind / an' t' grant my closet thoughts backyard / it is not of me t' sit an' ponder / wonderin' an' wastin' time."

Past interviews with our singer-songwriter, as shown by the excerpts in the prior section, make quite clear that Dylan himself does not wish to impose his own "foreign thoughts" on something that had issued from his imagination or intuition once-upon-a-time. Why dissect a piece of reverie or revelation with the surgical knife of reason when we can still "dance beneath the diamond sky with one hand waving free"? As far as our consideration here of the attempt by a philosopher to rationalize such phrases as "the foggy ruins of time" or "skippin' reels of rhyme," Dylan seems to inform us: "I wouldn't pay it any mind / It's just a shadow you're seein' that he's chasing" ("Mr. Tambourine Man"). Shadows are very much like abstract thoughts or ideas: intangible and yet shaped by a tangible reality.

Dylan suggests at times that he is a poet "in a destitute time" (to use Hölderlin's phrase) if only we were to look around, which Dylan certainly urges us to do in many of his songs. More and more works of popular culture—along with the everyday experiences of many who are sensitive enough to note that "the times, they are a-changin'"—point to a growing concern with the nihilistic dangers of despair, indifference, alienation, and fragmentation. *Nihilism* is an attitude that signals a collapse of values and a general feeling that "nothing matters." And among those who stroll along the "desolation rows" of contemporary culture, there seems to be an important role for the observant poet and his lines that sometimes rhyme.

Dylan's recognition of the tendency toward nihilism that haunts our age is clear not only in his lyrics, but also in certain non-musical remarks. For instance, in the *Biograph* notes to "Every Grain of Sand," he observes in biblical fashion:

> Everything is crooked now and the signs all point you the wrong way—it's like we're living at the time of the Tower of Babel, all our tongues are confused . . . It's a messy situation. People are just out parading around in disguises, wearing faces that don't let you know what they think.[12]

---

[12] *Biograph*, liner notes.

Dylan demonstrates that there is indeed a significant role for the poet, an individual who indicates that "things have changed," and not always for the better. One cannot help but detect in many of Dylan's songs a wistful and nostalgic glance back to the Woody Guthrie-Pete Seeger-Charlie Patton era of communities forged in the heat of golden prairies, back to a world that had not yet replaced its dustbowl determination with Super Bowl superficiality. A romantic sense of the "way things used to be" seems to inform Dylan's critical sense of "the way things are." As he also states in the *Biograph* notes to "Every Grain of Sand": "People like to talk about the new image of America but to me it's still the old one—Marlon Brando, James Dean, Marilyn Monroe, it's not computers, cocaine, and David Letterman, we gotta get off that—Hedy Lamarr, Dorothy Dandridge, that's my idea of America . . . and who's improved on it?"

Dylan is not so much a prophet, then, gazing forward into the future, as he is a smirking antiquary. And his capacity to appreciate as well as to borrow stealthily from a cozy yesteryear of mountain folk songs and city minstrel tunes is evident in the very title of one of his most recent albums: "*Love and Theft*". But amidst the nostalgia, there is certainly a subtle wisdom that warns us against repeating mistakes that have led others to horror or despair.

Dylan was one of the few singers not to have spoken out glibly about the tragedy of 9/11 (his album "*Love and Theft*" was actually released on that tragic day of 2001). If anything, he has been singing about the "darkness visible" in human existence since the early days. And perhaps that is the purpose or function of the poet in a destitute time. Think of the chilling question at the end of "The Ballad of Donald White" or the vicious racism of "The Death of Emmett Till" or the fear of death that permeates "I'd Hate to Be You on That Dreadful Day." Consider the dislocation of "Mixed Up Confusion" or the ruthless cynicism of "Masters of War" or the apocalyptic ruminations of "A Hard Rain's A-Gonna Fall." Contemplate the bleak fatalism of "Ballad of Hollis Brown" or the weary sarcasm of "With God on Our Side" or the outright nihilism of "Everything Is Broken." Or take Dylan's recent masterwork *Time Out of Mind*, an album that consistently evokes alienation and disorientation and shattered love in a "world gone wrong." And near the midpoint of his follow-up album "*Love and Theft*", the sense of doom and disorientation takes on diluvial dimensions when he tells us, like Noah peering out over the deck of his ark, that "[t]hings are breakin' up out there" because there's "[h]igh water everywhere" ("High Water [For Charlie Patton]").

While the true poet may not be able to cure or heal, he or she may at least be able to teach and comfort. That may be true of the philosopher as well, but to a different degree of effectiveness and emotional expressiveness. The genuine poet indicates the sickness and the danger so that we can find our own way out of the wilderness. The philosopher points to the darkness and makes us reflect upon it, but the poet has the potential to make us *feel* the darkness.

If our world has, at least in part, become "destitute" in terms of our increasing loss of feeling and imagination, as some critics of our postmodern age have suggested, the poet certainly has a role in reminding us why it is important to "dwell poetically," with mind and heart open to the horizon but with feet planted in the world of concrete objects and individuals. If our culture has become something of a nihilistic junk-heap in which *nothing matters* because *everything seems to matter*—the important and the trivial mixed together, as Dylan suggests in "Highway 61 Revisited"—then someone like Dylan must be there to point out that we are, in fact, standing amidst the wasteland. He may do so simply by standing on the junk-heap and throwing meaningless relics past our eyes.

This is not to say, of course, that Dylan does not simply have fun in his songs at times. There are many phrases and lines that merely serve the purpose, as far as I can tell, of re-working an old cliché or joke in a humorous way, or of merely cavorting along the contours of language. When you listen to a catchy tune such as "Jokerman" from the album *Infidels*, for example, the rhythm and sound of the spoken words outweigh any traces of a message or narrative. The world seems right when your foot is tapping and you are dancing "to the nightingale tune." Why the need to philosophize? And isn't Dylan himself the "jokerman" at times, trying to pull a fast one occasionally, suggesting depth when all he is doing is skipping along the surface of syllables? If so, we might temper the intensity of our philosophical laser beam at such moments—as Plato does, for instance, in his famous dialogue *The Symposium*, when his comically immoderate character Aristophanes begins to hiccough and cannot give his speech on the nature of *eros* or love. It's comic relief—and nothing more.

Often, in fact, it's the lyrics which seem to evade analysis so intentionally that belong to the most powerfully poetic of Dylan's songs. Philosophy typically strives for the clarity of definition and proposition. Poetry, in most cases, revels in ambiguity and mystery. Dylan's hymnal "Lay Down Your Weary Tune" comes to mind here, along with "Mr. Tambourine Man." What is there left for the philosopher to say with breezes blowing like bugles "[a]gainst the drums of dawn" and ocean waves crashing "like cymbals clashed." Here we are in the realm of "irreducible particulars," as a philosopher might put it: the realm of people and things and events that are so unique and individual that they do not lend themselves easily to generic conceptualization or analysis without losing their very individuality and richness of detail. It's the mystery that counts.

"The Foggy Ruins of Time"

In most of his songs, Dylan forces his attentive listener into ambiguous areas of restless mood and bursting image, areas that point out the limits of reflection and that therefore resist the power of reason. These regions prompt us to consider the very borderline between serious thought and sheer wonder. That is why philosophizing about Dylan's lyrics is, at times, like trying to jump from one ocean wave to another. The intersections between the melodic sounds of his words and the images or thoughts that those words summon tend to crest, break, and pass before one can gain a firm foothold. (But who would try to walk on water anyway?)

The most revealing, and ironic, fact about many of Dylan's songs, perhaps, is that the ambiguity which emerges from his wordplay seduces us into trying to generalize or universalize something that resists this very attempt. In this sense, the ambiguity that is produced by the attempt to capture an absolutely unique, and thus un-definable, person, event, or emotion echoes in some strange fashion the ambiguity that emanates from a purely abstract idea or thought. And there is a mysterious and difficult pathway that seems to lead from one level to another. This is the pathway, possibly, where poetry and philosophy meet, having embarked from different corners of the forest. As Ricks puts it in *Dylan's Visions of Sin*: "[A]ny general praises of Dylan's art are sure to miss what matters most about it: that it is not general, but highly and deeply individual, particular. This, while valuing human commonalty."[13]

For example, "Lay, Lady, Lay" is not really a song about the nature of romance or love in general, though some who are philosophically minded might tend to interpret it as such. Nor is it a song about the presence of lustful desire in the heart of every adult male. Rather, it is a song that is sung by a *very specific* man and addressed in a *very specific* way and with a *very specific* tone or feeling to a *very specific* lady. No names are used, but that doesn't matter. The inescapable particularity of the song resides in the voice, the words, and the music. It is therefore a song that is closer to the true nature of love, in a way, than any abstract intellectual explanation could afford. And yet the song forces us to ponder the meaning of love just the same, *in spite of* the air of specificity and individuality that is conjured.

Thus reason's pursuit of clarity and understanding is sparked by the resistance of that which lies beyond reason's boundaries. Poetry occasions mystery and, subsequently, the very sense of wonder in which philosophy is typically initiated. There's something to be said, at the end of the day, for the importance of mood and image—of that which is inherently non-philosophical and poetic—in explaining how we come to experience and to inquire philosophically about the world as well as about ourselves.

---

[13] Ricks, *Visions*, p. 20.

The Bob Dylan Discography

Bob Dylan	1962
The Freewheelin' Bob Dylan	1963
The Times They Are A-Changin'	1964
Another Side of Bob Dylan	1964
Bringing It All Back Home	1965
Highway 61 Revisited	1965
Blonde on Blonde	1966
Bob Dylan's Greatest Hits	1967
John Wesley Harding	1967
Nashville Skyline	1969
Self Portrait	1970
New Morning	1970
Bob Dylan's Greatest Hits, Volume 2	1971
Pat Garrett and Billy the Kid	1973
Dylan	1973
Planet Waves	1974
Before the Flood	1974
Blood on the Tracks	1975
The Basement Tapes	1975
Desire	1976
Hard Rain	1976
Street Legal	1978
At Budokan	1979
Slow Train Coming	1979
Saved	1980
Shot of Love	1981
Infidels	1983
Real Live	1984
Empire Burlesque	1985
Biograph	1985
Knocked Out Loaded	1986
Dylan & the Dead	1988
Down in the Groove	1988

Oh Mercy	1989
Under the Red Sky	1990
The Bootleg Series Volumes 1-3	1991
Good as I Been to You	1992
The 30th Anniversary Concert Celebration	1993
World Gone Wrong	1993
Bob Dylan's Greatest Hits, Volume 3	1994
MTV Unplugged	1995
Time Out of Mind	1997
Live 1966	1998
The Essential Bob Dylan	2000
"Love and Theft"	2001
Live 1975	2002
Live 1964	2004
No Direction Home: The Soundtrack	2005
Live at the Gaslight: 1962	2005

The Mongrel Dogs

DOUG ANDERSON teaches American philosophy and history of philosophy at Penn State. His most recent work, *Philosophy Americana*, deals with themes in American philosophy and popular culture. In his alterlife he plays Americana music. Having played in early years with singer-songwriters John Gorka and Richard Shindell, he now beats his Froggy Bottom and Oriskany guitars in the fourth-rate bars of rural Pennsylvania for rebels, refugees, rakes, and misdemeanor outlaws.

FRANCIS J. BECKWITH, ever since he was street legal, knew he had to strengthen the things that remain. That's why he became a philosopher (Ph.D., Fordham) and then went to law school (M.J.S., Washington University, St. Louis), where he learned that to live outside the law he must be honest. He is Associate Professor in, and Associate Director of, the J.M. Dawson Institute of Church-State Studies, and Associate Professor of Church-State Studies at Baylor University, where they have Charles Darwin trapped on Highway 35. In 2002–03, he was a Visiting Fellow in Politics at Princeton University, where the locusts sang their high whining trill. His wife, Frankie, is his precious angel who can do the Georgia crawl.

ANAT BILETZKI is Professor of Philosophy at Tel Aviv University. She specializes in philosophy of language and its history, and has published books on logic, paradoxes, Hobbes, and Wittgenstein. Of no less significance for her is her work on human rights in Israel-Palestine, which has taught her much about those who have God on their side.

ELIZABETH BRAKE is assistant professor of philosophy at the University of Calgary. Her research interests are in ethics, political philosophy, and feminism. She has published articles on Kant and Hegel on marriage, on liberal neutrality, and on fathers' rights. Elizabeth doesn't have everything she needs.

MICHAEL CHIARELLO is dean of Clare College and professor of philosophy at St. Bonaventure University. He has published articles on applied ethics, ethical skepticism, political radicalism, and curriculum development. An amateur inventor, he holds patents for the disposable necktie, the sport utility row boat and the pedestrian airbag. His mind is filled with big ideas, images, and assorted snacks.

RUVIK DANIELI is a freelance writer-translator-editor based in Israel. He has worked in movie screenwriting, video productions, CD-rom and internet projects, fiction and poetry, philosophical dissertations, art catalogues and sundry other varieties of textual endeavor. He might yet become a singer-songwriter, and is most proud of having kept his head out of a guillotine this long.

RICK ANTHONY FURTAK is Assistant Professor of Philosophy at Colorado College. He is the author of *Wisdom in Love: Kierkegaard and the Ancient Quest for Emotional Integrity* (2005) and a variety of other publications in philosophy and literature. Since he was only a few days old when *Blood on the Tracks* was released in 1975, he grew up thinking that Woodstock was only a character in the Sunday comics.

DAVID GOLDBLATT is Professor of Philosophy at Denison University in Ohio. He is the author of *Art and Ventriloquism* in Routledge's Critical Voices Series. With Lee B. Brown, he is co-editor of *Aesthetics: A Reader in the Philosophy of the Arts*. He has also published widely on the subjects of art and philosophy, with articles notably in *The Journal of Aesthetics and Art Criticism, Philosophy and Film, The Southern Journal of Philosophy, Philosophy and Literature,* and *Art Issues* among many others. Recently, Goldblatt was photographed in Bob Dylan's childhood bathtub. The tub was purchased on EBay by the small Boston design firm Bis Bis; the photograph is slated to appear in a book for a charitable cause.

THEODORE GRACYK was fourth row center at one of the Warfield Theater performances of November 1979. Since then, he's moved to a little Minnesota town where he teaches philosophy and writes about the aesthetics of music. He has published two books, *Rhythm and Noise: An Aesthetics of Rock* and *I Wanna Be Me: Rock Music and the Politics of Identity*. His next book is on musical taste. In his spare time, he writes the jokes that Bob tells between songs.

JAMES C. KLAGGE is Professor of Philosophy at Virginia Tech. He teaches a wide range of courses including Ancient Greek culture, ethics, political theory, and contemporary analytic philosophy. The author of some twenty articles and editor of four books, his research recently has centered on Ludwig Wittgenstein (1889–1951), probably the most influential philosopher of the last hundred years. In addition to being an academic philosopher, Jim has published a dozen op-ed pieces, run several marathons, served as an elected school board member for eight years, and become a certified mediator for juvenile and domestic relations cases. His first "encounter" with Bob Dylan came at age fourteen when he was reading something aloud in class and unknowingly mispronounced Bob's last name as "Die-lyn." He's been trying to make up for it ever since.

AVERY KOLERS is a pawn in the Philosophy Department at the University of Louisville.

KEVIN KREIN is an Associate Professor of Philosophy at the University of Alaska Southeast. In Southeast Alaska the hard rain often falls, the snowflakes often storm, and Kevin often spends his evenings philosophizing, listening to Bob Dylan, and considering the depth of the rain, the snow, and Dylan's lyrics.

ABIGAIL LEVIN is currently completing a Ph.D. in philosophy at the University of Toronto. She has been philosophizing about Bob Dylan since the age of thirteen, and she firmly believes that the correct answer to the question of "If you were stranded on a desert island with only one Dylan album, what would it be?" is *Bringing It All Back Home*.

PAUL LULEWICZ studied philosophy at Marquette University, where he started out on burgundy, and the University of Wisconsin, where he soon hit the harder stuff. He currently works as a free lance writer and editor in Japan. For him, this book is personal; it's not (thankfully) about the loot.

EDWARD NECARSULMER is a literary agent in his native home of Manhattan. He has an undergraduate degree in Philosophy from Denison University and continues to disprove the notion that philosophy majors don't get jobs. Edward has lived on 3rd Street and can often be found at the grand canyon, at sundown.

CARL J. PORTER is the Executive Director of Academic Support Services and Programs at Weber State University. He also teaches in the English Department and the Honors Program but as soon as the axe falls, he is off to New Orleans. He co-directs the National Undergraduate Literature Conference and co-edited *The Peregrine Reader*, a collection of writings by the conferences' featured speakers. He lives in Ogden, Utah, where there is little music in the cafes at night and no revolution in the air.

Jordy Rocheleau is an assistant professor of philosophy at Austin Peay State University in Clarksville, Tennessee. Taught and brought up in the Midwest, he completed his Ph.D. at Michigan State University with a dissertation titled "Universalism and Its Critics: A Defense of Discourse Ethics." Liberal to a degree, he has published papers in democratic theory and environmental ethics, and is currently writing a book on ethics in education and researching international ethics. Though skeptical about following wandering tambourine players or pigeon-covered Eskimos, Jordy is interested in dancing over the graves of warmongers and cheek to cheek in Mozambique.

James S. Spiegel is Professor of Philosophy and Religion at Taylor University. His books include *Hypocrisy: Moral Fraud and Other Vices* (1999) and *How to be Good in a World Gone Bad* (2004). He has published numerous articles on issues in ethics, aesthetics, and philosophy of religion. Jim is also a guitarist who writes and records his own music. When he is not teaching, writing or recording, he spends his time (outside the Gates of Eden) discussing what's real and what is not.

Kevin L. Stoehr teaches Humanities at Boston University. He has contributed essays to *The Sopranos and Philosophy* (2004) and *Movies and the Meaning of Life* (2005). He is the author of the forthcoming book *Nihilism in Film and Television* and has edited the collection *Film and Knowledge* (2002). While he has never philosophized disgrace or stood in line for a Gregory Peck movie or stayed in Mississippi a day too long, he has also never painted a masterpiece . . . nor sketched a waitress on a napkin, for that matter. Well, not yet, but he's getting there.

Martin Van Hees is professor of ethics at the Faculty of Philosophy of the University of Groningen, Netherlands. He has published two books and numerous articles on moral and political theories of freedom. His interest in Dylan started when he was fourteen years old and heard the album *Street Legal*. He didn't have a clue as to what it was all about, yet found it highly captivating and illuminating, a response to Dylan's work that still persists.

Peter Vernezze is an Associate Professor of Philosophy at Weber State University in Ogden, Utah, although he has not managed to build a cabin there, nor to marry even one wife, nor to catch many trout. He co-edited the volume *The Sopranos and Philosophy* and published the Stoic self-help manual *Don't Worry, Be Stoic: Ancient Wisdom for Troubled Times*.

Reciting the Alphabet